# SECRET
# SUSSEX

*Ellie Seymour*
*Photos by Lyndsey Haskell*

JONGLEZ PUBLISHING
travel guides

Ellie Seymour is a travel writer, blogger and author of *Secret Brighton: An Unusual Guide*, also published by Jonglez. She writes about all things unusual and unique travel on her blog, Ellie & Co (www.ellieandco.co.uk) and is always looking for the next adventure. She cannot walk past an intriguing alleyway or courtyard without seeing what's on the other side – and has a weakness for overgrown graveyards and bizarre local museums. She was born a London girl but has lived in Brighton for fifteen years.

We have taken great pleasure in drawing up *Secret Sussex* and hope that through its guidance you will, like us, continue to discover unusual, hidden or little-known aspects of the region.
Descriptions of certain places are accompanied by thematic sections highlighting historical details or anecdotes as an aid to understanding the region in all its complexity. *Secret Sussex* also draws attention to the multitude of details found in places that we may pass every day without noticing.
These are an invitation to look more closely at the urban landscape and, more generally, a means of seeing our own region with the curiosity and attention that we often display while travelling else-where ...

Comments on this guidebook and its contents, as well as information on places we may not have mentioned, are more than welcome and will enrich future editions.

Don't hesitate to contact us:
E-mail: info@jonglezpublishing.com
Jonglez Publishing, 25 rue du Maréchal Foch
78000 Versailles, France

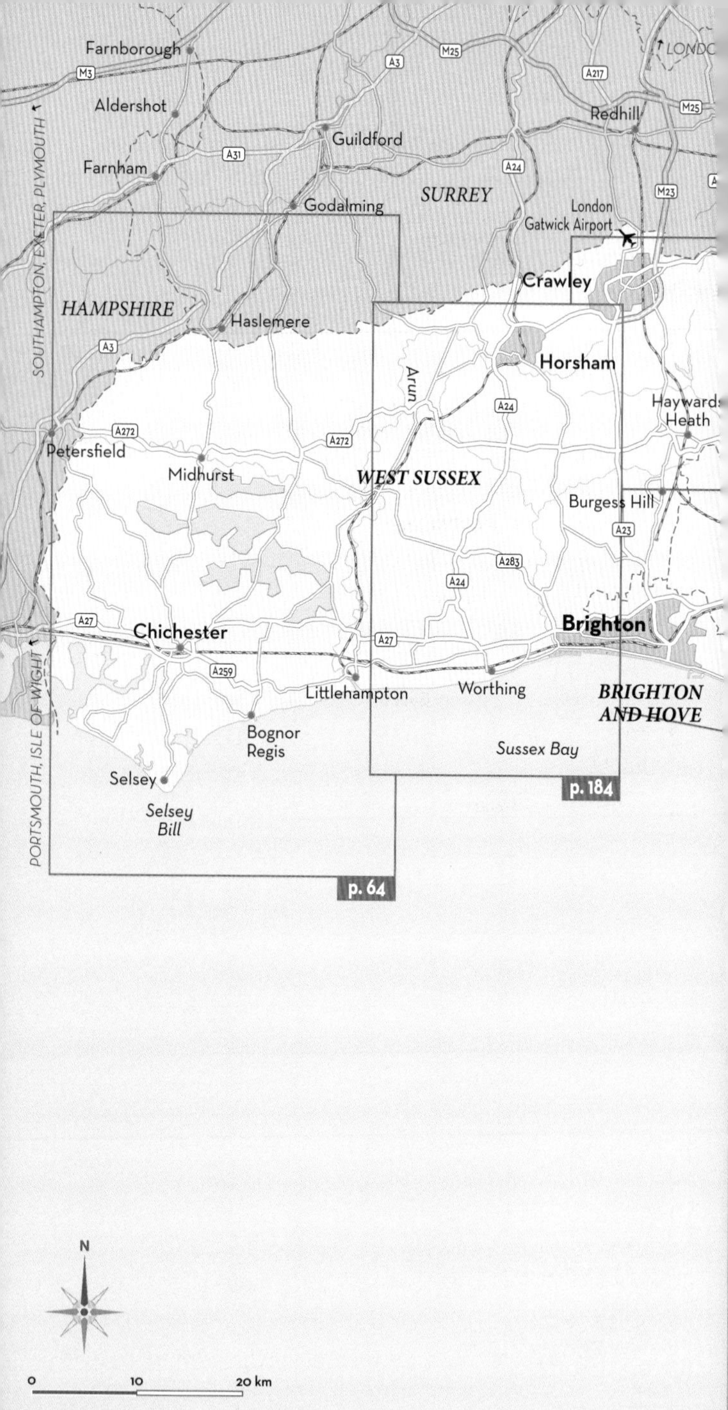

Farnborough
Aldershot
Guildford
Farnham
Godalming
SURREY
Redhill
London
LONDON
London Gatwick Airport
Crawley
HAMPSHIRE
Haslemere
Horsham
Arun
Haywards Heath
Petersfield
Midhurst
WEST SUSSEX
Burgess Hill
Brighton
Chichester
Littlehampton
Worthing
BRIGHTON AND HOVE
Bognor Regis
Sussex Bay
Selsey
Selsey Bill
SOUTHAMPTON, EXETER, PLYMOUTH
PORTSMOUTH, ISLE OF WIGHT
M3
M25
M23
A3
A217
A31
A24
A272
A27
A259
A283
A23
p. 64
p. 184
N
0
10
20 km

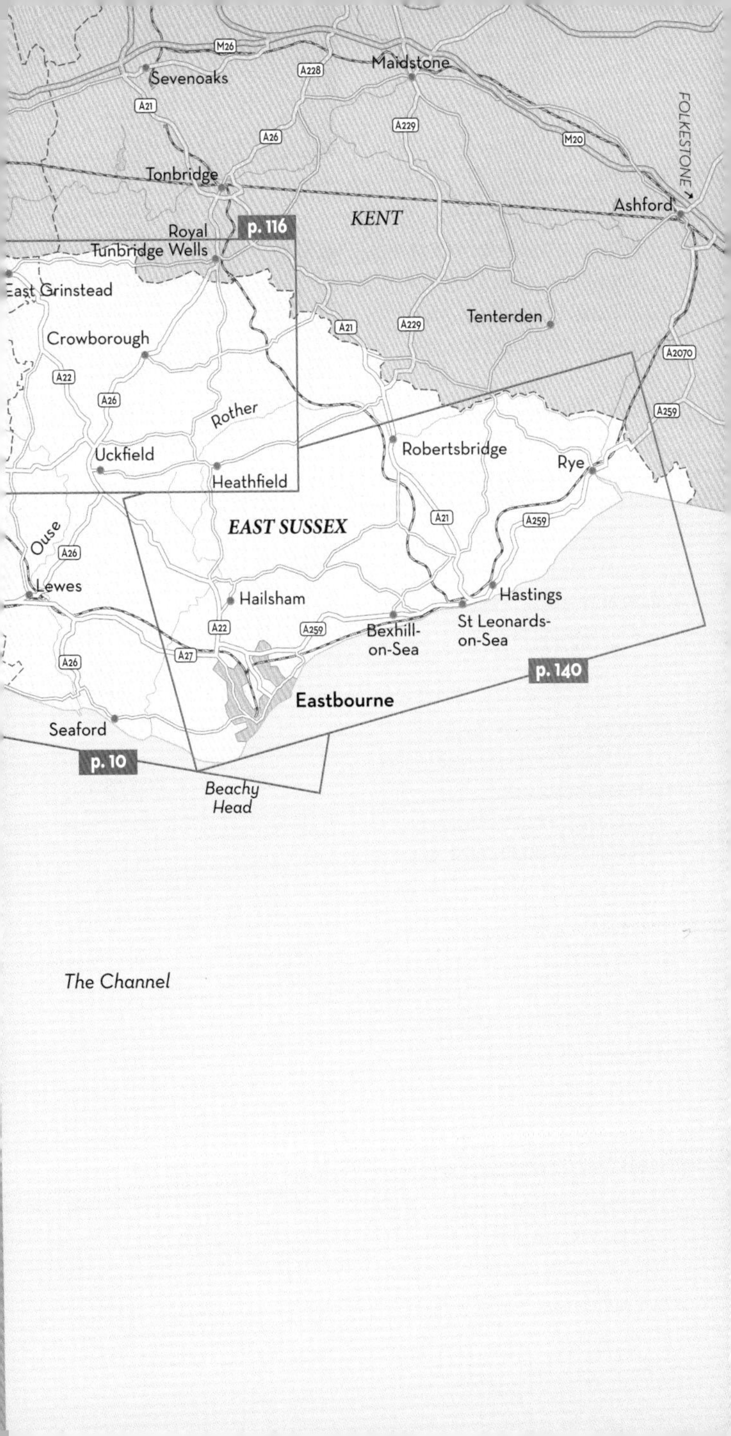

M26
Sevenoaks
A228
Maidstone
A21
A229
A26
M20
FOLKESTONE
Tonbridge
Ashford
KENT
p. 116
Royal Tunbridge Wells
East Grinstead
Tenterden
A21
A229
Crowborough
A2070
A22
A26
Rother
A259
Robertsbridge
Uckfield
Heathfield
Rye
EAST SUSSEX
A21
A259
Ouse
A26
Lewes
Hailsham
Hastings
St Leonards-on-Sea
A22
A259
Bexhill-on-Sea
A27
A26
p. 140
Eastbourne
Seaford
p. 10
Beachy Head
The Channel

# CONTENTS

## *Burgess Hill to Seaford*



## *Chichester to Petworth*

## *Crawley to Crowborough*

# CONTENTS



## *Eastbourne to Rye*



## *Horsham to Worthing*

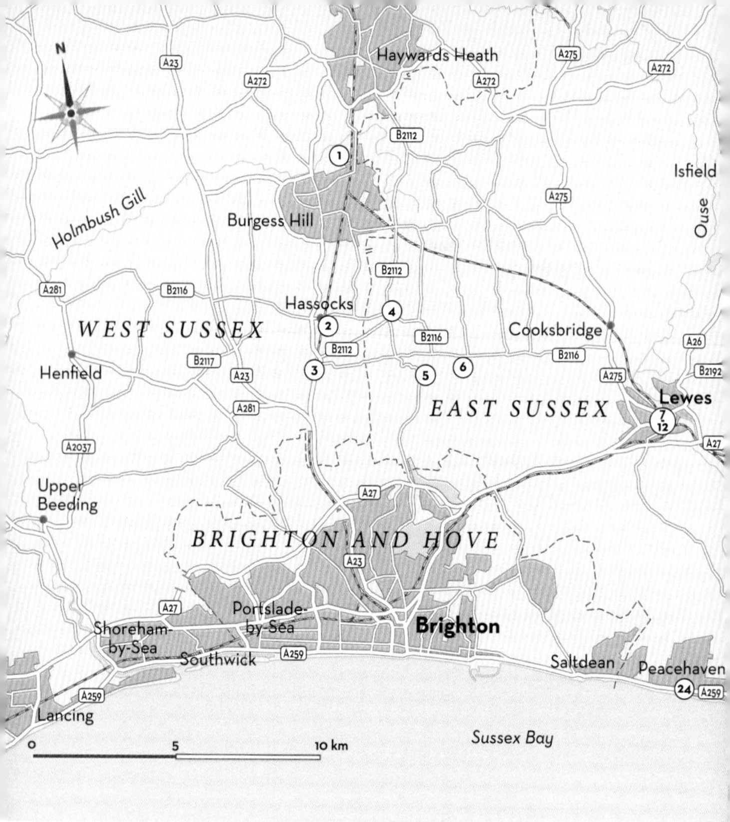


# *Burgess Hill to Seaford*

---

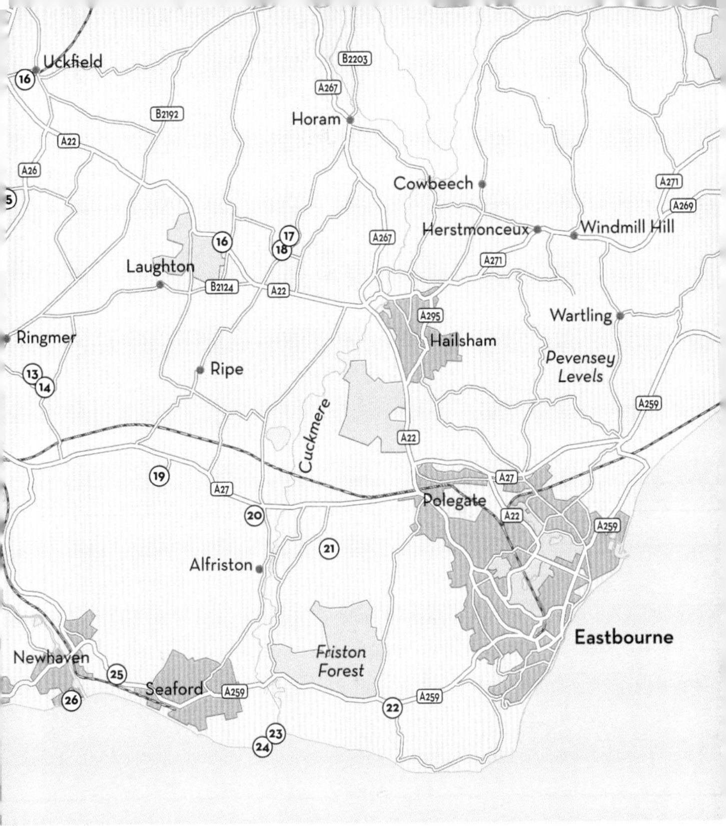
Uckfield
B2203
A267
B2192
Horam
A22
A26
Cowbeech
A271
A269
Herstmonceux
Windmill Hill
A267
Laughton
A271
B2124
A22
Wartling
A295
Ringmer
Hailsham
Pevensey Levels
Ripe
A259
Cuckmere
A22
A27
Polegate
A27
A22
A259
Alfriston
Eastbourne
Friston Forest
Newhaven
Seaford
A259
A259

# GREEN CIRCLE PUBLIC ART TRAIL

①

## *An ode to the town's forgotten local inhabitants*

*At various green spaces around Burgess Hill, East Sussex*
*burgesshill.gov.uk/greencircle*

A network of paths, cycle tracks and bridleways linked to the town centre, the Burgess Hill Green Circle was created to encourage locals to rediscover their town's greenspaces.

It recently became the setting for an intriguing art trail that pays tribute to the incredible lives and significant achievements of the area's forgotten inhabitants.

There are five sculptures in total to find on the trail, each one located within a different setting on the outskirts of town – Grassmere Meadow, Malthouse Lane Meadows, Hammonds Ridge Meadows, Nightingale Lane Meadows, and Bedelands Farm Local Nature Reserve. Each one is clearly marked on a map inside a trail leaflet which you can download from the link opposite.

For example, a search for the Flow of Life Boundary Markers by Janine Creaye, takes you to Bedelands Farm Nature Reserve to discover two striking hand-carved sculptures. They represent the incredible diversity within its meadows, often overlooked in favour of the nearby South Downs, yet home to wildflowers so rare their seeds are stored in the vaults of the Millennium Seed Bank (see p. 124).

Meanwhile, an ode to a little-known local filmmaker, explorer and naturalist, called John Charles Bee Mason, finds you at Hammonds Ridge Meadows on the other side of town. During his incredible career, he worked as a First World War photographer, a cinematographer on various scientific expeditions, including Shackleton's final voyage to the Antarctic, and travelled across the Bolivian jungle. As an enthusiastic apiarist, he also made films about beekeeping. His life and work are commemorated in a mosaic film reel created by local artist, Alan Potter.

Elsewhere, another sculpture on the trail called *Bluebird Contained*, by Steve Geliot, celebrates the ground-breaking design and engineering work of Ken and Lew Norris – known as the Norris Brothers. Together they were responsible for the design of Donald Campbell's *Bluebird* hydroplane and *Bluebird* car, which between them set eight world records, including a water-speed record, and a land-speed record.

Also on the trail, former local resident, Emily Temple, a successful 19th-century businesswoman and philanthropist is commemorated for gifting various parks and buildings to Burgess Hill.

# MUSEUM OF GARDENING ②

*A marvellous collection of mowers*

*South Downs Heritage Centre*
*South Downs Nurseries, Brighton Road, Hassocks, East Sussex, BN6 9LY*
*01273 847707*
*southdownsheritagecentre.co.uk/museum*
*Monday to Saturday 9am–5.30pm, Sunday 10.00am–4.30pm*
*Admission free*

Connected to the vast South Downs Nurseries in Hassocks, the South Downs Heritage Centre hides a compact and quirky museum devoted to the history of gardening.

It was set up by Clive Gravett, a local man with a family background in horticulture, farming and conservation, to promote his charity, the Budding Foundation which raises money to help disadvantaged young people. It is not surprising to learn that Gravett – a self-described lawnmower historian – named the charity after Edwin Beard Budding, the inventor of the lawnmower.

The museum aims to tell the story of modern gardening from the mid-1800s up to the present day. As you would expect, it boasts an impressive collection of restored lawnmowers, not to mention other gardening tools and machinery, all in immaculate condition despite their age – some machines date back to the late 1800s.

Gravett sources his finds from various places, such as auctions, online auctions and donations. "Most pieces I find often date back to the 1950s and 60s, but occasionally I'll stumble on something rare, like three mowers I recently collected from Portslade in Brighton, one of which dates from 1881. That doesn't happen often!" says Gravett.

The museum is organised into clearly marked sections – from watering and spraying, to pruning and lawn mowing. Each one featuring restored gardening equipment and information boards peppered with interesting snippets. For example, "Terracotta" showcases local garden pottery and tile work made in Burgess Hill, once a centre for potteries and brickworks. The Keymer Tile Works was the last of its kind in the area, and closed in 2014.

Elsewhere, there is a section on the Sussex "trug" basket – of which Meryl Streep is apparently a fan, according to one anecdote. These wooden baskets are handmade by master trug makers who train for five years and can only become fully qualified when they can proficiently make all eight types of trug.

Meanwhile, children particularly love watching bees at work in their transparent hive in the poignant "Love the bees" section, which teaches us to look after this endangered species.

Outside, yet more retro machinery fills the terrace by the entrance, going right up to the café, and includes two old Massey tractors from the mid-1950s.

If you cannot get enough of old lawnmowers and gardening equipment, you will find another smaller exhibition similar to this one in the courtyard of Leonardslee Gardens, also curated by the Budding Foundation (see p. 188 and p. 190).

# CLAYTON TUNNEL NORTH PORTAL ③

## *How to make an entrance*

*Clayton Hill, Clayton, East Sussex, BN6 9PQ*
*For a tour of the single-storey cottage on the top of the castle: heritageopendays.org.uk*

Five miles north of Brighton close to the small village of Clayton in East Sussex is a railway tunnel carved into the South Downs.

It looks different to most with its elaborate design, given that its north entrance resembles a miniature castle, complete with two grand turrets. This is what is known as a "folly", an extravagant architectural feature popular in Victorian times, added purely for decoration and usually with no practical purpose. However, just how this one came to be added to one end of the Clayton Tunnel remains a mystery.

Rumours abound, the first relating to the tunnel itself, which was built in 1841 as part of the London and South Coast Railway, linking the then up-and-coming seaside town of Brighton to London. Some believe the castle-like structure was added after the tunnel was complete, as a monument to this feat of engineering and to the 6,000 men who spent three years digging through 2,000 metres of chalk hills in terrible conditions.

Another theory relates to passenger experience: in the 1800s, steam train travel was a relatively new technology and many people at the time (although excited about progress) were also fearful of it. It has been suggested that it was added as a way of reassuring nervous passengers entering the tunnel for the first time that they were not about to descend into the depths of Hell.

The most plausible answer, however, is that it was added as a way of appeasing the local landowner and convincing him to allow the tunnel to be dug in the first place.

Adding to this bizarre railway tunnel's intriguing nature, is the sight of the small single-storey cottage on the top of the castle. This was added nine years later as a home for the signalman and his family. It was his job to light oil lamps along the tunnel for guiding trains through. Today, it is a private home and occasionally open for tours during Heritage Open Days.

## *A ghost story*

As well as whimsical architecture, the Clayton Tunnel was also the site of a serious accident now referred to as The Clayton Tunnel Railway Crash. On 25 August 1861, 23 people lost their lives and 176 were injured after a signalling failure. Since it happened, sightings of two ghostly figures walking hand in-hand into the entrance of the tunnel have been reported. The incident and related sightings are thought to have provided inspiration for Charles Dickens' ghost story, *The Signalman.*

# BROWNE BURIAL GROUND

④

*A mysterious private miniature cemetery*

*The Twitten, Ditchling, East Sussex*
*24/7*

Tucked away up a narrow alleyway in the East Sussex village of Ditchling, the Browne Burial Ground is a fascinating miniature graveyard packed with headstones. It is not only bizarre due to its diminutive size, but also its location: you will find it sandwiched between a cottage and the front garden of a house built many years later.

The fact it is set apart from the much larger and more spacious churchyard opposite belonging to the Old Meeting Place (also known as the Ditchling Unitarian Church) only adds to its intrigue.

It is thought that the idea to create it was that of a local man called Peter Browne who, around 1760, is said to have set aside a part of what was then his garden as a private burial place for his family. When he died, the rest of his land passed into other hands.

To make sure the burial ground could be accessed, he bought the strip of land down to East End Lane, which now forms part of The Twitten.

There are lots of references to the Browne family in the chapel records, including this one about James Browne: "An outstanding member of the period 1790-1834 was James Browne, a Ditchling grocer, who lived at Place House, the timbered Tudor building opposite the Church now called Wings Place".

## *Twitten: "a path between two walls or hedges"*

The setting for this curious graveyard along a narrow alleyway, known as a twitten, is a curiosity in itself. Twittens are distinguishing features of many Sussex towns. An old Sussex dictionary dating back to 1875 describes them as "a narrow path between two walls or hedges" – yet its origins are unclear. Reports suggest it derives from the Anglo-Saxon word *twicen*, meaning a place where two roads meet, or *twitchel*, a word used in the north Midlands in the 14th century to mean a forked road. It is also often said to relate to the words 'betwixt' and 'between'. There are some twittens to discover in Lewes as well as Brighton, where it was once possible to walk through them from one side of Brighton's 'Old Town' to the other (see *Secret Brighton: An Unusual Guide*, from the same publisher, for more details).

## *Victorian oddities*

At the other end of The Twitten, the bizarre black pipe sticking out of the ground is a ventilation pipe: a piece of Victorian design and engineering whose function is much less fascinating than its intricate design. There are two more examples to discover in the village, including one in East Gardens.

# DARK SKY SITES

⑤

## *Seeing stars in Sussex*

*South Downs National Park*
*East and West Sussex*
*southdowns.gov.uk/communicating-south-downs/dark-night-skies/south-downs-dark-sky-discovery-sites/*

Light pollution from streetlights, neon signs and industrial lighting makes it hard to get a good clear view of the night sky. But in recent years, several places around the UK have been recognised as great places to stargaze without the light pollution.

The South Downs National Park in Sussex is one of these landscapes. It was awarded International Dark Sky Reserve status in 2016 by the US-based International Dark Sky Association, along with the Brecon Beacons National Park in Wales, and Exmoor National Park in Devon.

Meanwhile, a similar initiative run by the UK Dark Sky Discovery partnership – a network of astronomy and open space organisations which aim to encourage people to stargaze – recognises various Dark Sky Discovery Sites within these reserves, of which there are plenty in the South Downs National Park.

In Sussex, these include Ditchling Beacon, Devil's Dyke, Birling Gap and Bignor Hill. These places are recognised as great spots for seeing stars in the night sky with either the naked eye or a good pair of binoculars. They also have excellent public access.

Gaining either Dark Sky Reserve or Dark Sky Site status involves a lengthy and rigorous application process. It requires the ability to demonstrate local authority commitment to lighting policies, public education and community involvement.

## *Dark Skies Festival*

To help encourage and introduce people to stargazing in Sussex, every year the South Downs National Park and other venues around the county take part in the Dark Skies Festival. This runs for two weeks and includes events, talks and activities aimed at anyone wanting to enjoy or learn more about the night sky.

To find out more, visit darkskiesnationalparks.org.uk

Stargazers keen to take their interest in astronomy to another level, will appreciate a visit to the Observatory Science Centre for the chance to see the night sky through a 26-inch telescope, originally used when the building was the Royal Observatory Greenwich headquarters. See p. 154 for further information.

# QUEEN VICTORIA JUBILEE PLANTATION

⑥

## *A striking natural landmark*

*Streat Down*
*Near Plumpton, South Downs National Park, East Sussex*

Next time you are hiking around the East Sussex countryside near the villages of Streat, Plumpton or Ditchling, cast your eye up to an escarpment on the north face of the South Downs known as Streat Down.

Here, you will notice a neatly arranged clump of trees set out in the shape of a "V". It stretches almost from the top to the bottom of the escarpment, and can be seen from lots of different vantage points in the area. A particularly good viewing spot is at the south end of Streat Lane.

Planted in 1887 for Queen Victoria's Golden Jubilee (which celebrated 50 years since she came to the throne in 1837) this natural landmark is what is known locally as the Queen Victoria Jubilee Plantation.

It is said to have originally been created out of 3,000 beech, fir and lime trees, some of which had to be replanted in 1918 due to damage. It is still regularly maintained to this day.

On 20 June 1987, to mark 100 years since it was planted, a local man called Mr Rudebeck organised a celebratory picnic on the site for villagers. It took place 100 years to the day after Queen Victoria's Golden Jubilee was celebrated in 1887, although then there was the slightly more formal event of a banquet for European kings and princes.

## NEARBY

### *The Plumpton Cross*

On the same escarpment of the South Downs, to the left of the Queen Victoria Jubilee Plantation, the Plumpton Cross is carved into the chalk hillside and can be seen only in the right light. Its origins are not known, but it is thought to be a reminder of the spot where Simon de Montfort assembled his army before defeating King Henry III at the Battle of Lewes on 14 May 1264.

### *A tasty hidden gem*

In the tiny village of Streat, behind the Elizabethan Manor house and Streat Parish Church, next to the entrance to The Dairy at Streat Place Barn, you will find a tasty hidden surprise – Suzy's Streat Food, a little honesty food stall, selling homemade cakes, jams and cordials.

# MERIDIAN LINE MARKERS

⑦

## *Where the east meets west*

*101a Western Road, Lewes, East Sussex*
*Open to view from the outside only*

Lewes is one of the Sussex towns through which the Greenwich meridian line runs, dividing the eastern and western hemispheres.

The Greenwich meridian line – also referred to as the prime meridian – is an imaginary line which runs from the North Pole to the South Pole through the main telescope at the Royal Observatory in Greenwich, London. This is the point of zero longitude, from which all other lines of longitude are measured.

In Lewes, there are three markers to find. Two are hidden in plain sight at the end of a row of terraced houses outside EE Goacher Antique Upholsterers near the junction of Western Road and Spital Road.

The first is a cast-iron plaque set into the pavement, designed like this so that passers-by who notice it can say they have stepped on the eastern and western hemispheres at the same time. The second is set into the wall just above it.

Both date to 1975, when the Royal Observatory Greenwich celebrated its 300th anniversary. Considering how many roads in Lewes the meridian crosses, it is a bit of a mystery as to why they were both placed so close together, although it is thought that other identical markers may have been set up elsewhere and were later lost.

The third marker in the town is an obelisk on Meridian Road, erected in 1938. There is a similar one on the promenade in Peacehaven.

The Royal Observatory Greenwich was chosen as the location for the prime meridian in 1884 after 41 delegates from 25 nations met in Washington, DC, for the International Meridian Conference. The decision, essentially, was based on the argument that by naming Greenwich the point of zero longitude, the position of the date line on the opposite side of the Earth would inconvenience the least number of people.

## *The Greenwich Meridian Trail*

A novel way to discover the meridian lines in Lewes and others around the country is to tackle the Greenwich Meridian Trail. This long-distance walk (440 km) follows the line of the Greenwich meridian through England. Created in 2009 to coincide with the 125th anniversary of the Greenwich meridian line, it starts in Peacehaven, East Sussex, and ends in Sand Le Mere, East Yorkshire. After 107 km, the walk passes directly through the prime meridian at the historic Royal Observatory in Greenwich, the headquarters of which were at one time located in East Sussex (see p. 154).

# FIRE + WILD OUTDOOR DINING EXPERIENCES ⑧

*Secret suppers in the forest*

*In the woods near Lewes,*
*East Sussex*
*fireandwild.co.uk*

Sussex is abundant with great restaurants offering innovative tasting menus, but none as exciting as Fire + Wild, a dining and events company – with a twist.

Every few months, they transform a secret woodland location close to their base in Lewes, East Sussex, into the magical setting for an epic intimate outdoor banquet, inspired by the seasons.

Adding to the intrigue, dinner guests do not find out the exact location of their feast until the day. Instead, they are given instructions to gather at a specific meeting place. From here, they follow a Fire + Wild team member through the forest where their table awaits, and the experience begins.

A five-course tasting menu is served at each 'wild dining' event, which is cooked over fire for guests to watch. Each dish is created using ingredients which are hunted, foraged and harvested from the surrounding landscape; for example, this might include organic meat, fresh line-caught fish, wild greens, berries and fungi.

Each dish is paired with wild cocktails and local wines and other infusions designed to complement the flavours of the food.

"The part I get most excited about is the storytelling", says chef, hunter and forager Mark Andrews, who set up Fire + Wild in 2017. "I love the challenge and creative process that comes with designing the menu, linking the courses together and connecting it all with the habitat or a particular season. Of course, the real reward comes from watching the excitement on guests' faces as the experience unfolds."

Mark set up the company after several chaotic years working in London. At this point, he decided it was time for a new start and to return to his rural roots for a simpler way of life. Once he had left London, he spent the next few years exploring the wild parts of Scotland, Sweden and France on remote camping and canoe trips, while foraging for food, hunting and cooking over fire.

As well as their outdoor dining experiences, they also organise guided foraging walks, wild camping trips and workshops on cooking with fire and making cocktails with foraged ingredients.

In keeping with their values, Fire + Wild also donate five per cent of their profits to The Woodland Trust each year, and they have a low impact, zero waste policy.

# PROTESTANT MARTYRS' PRISON STEPS ⑨

## *A sobering tribute*

*Town Hall*
*High Street, Lewes, East Sussex, BN7 2QS*
*Open to view from the outside only*

Outside Lewes Town Hall, a bizarre hole in the pavement is covered in glass with railings around it. Look closely and you will see that it covers a set of stone steps leading into the building's basement. They remind us of a gruesome period of time in Lewes' history.

Dating back to the 15th century, these steps once led into the vaults of the Old Star Inn, located where the Town Hall now stands. It was in these vaults that a group of 10 Protestant martyrs were imprisoned before they were led up the steps and burned at the stake a few yards from here on the High Street.

These martyrs were victims of what were known as the Marian Persecutions, instigated by Queen Mary Tudor, the eldest daughter of Henry VIII, who sought to reintroduce Catholicism when she succeeded her half-brother.

A total of 288 Protestants around the country were executed simply for their beliefs – 17 of them in Lewes. Those whom Mary chose to execute ranged from pregnant women to scholars, from the poor to the Archbishop of Canterbury, Thomas Cranmer.

The 10 Lewes martyrs were arrested during a prayer meeting at the home of a Brighton brewer called Deryk Carver. Some were taken to Newgate Prison in London, where they refused to deny their faith and were sentenced to burn.

Of the 10 prisoners – six men and four women – only two had been brought to trial. The others were apprehended two or three days before they were killed. Without any authority or writ of condemnation from the proper authorities, they were hurried to Lewes and burned together in one giant human bonfire, which subsequently turned the country against Queen Mary.

The steps were covered over until the recent renovation of the Lewes Town Hall façade. It was then decided to maximise the historical interest of the site and create a hole in the pavement on High Street, to allow people to see the steps that accompany the story of the martyrs, as told on a plaque outside the Town Hall.

## *Other reminders of the Marian Persecutions*

Lewes Bonfire Night was set up to mark Guy Fawkes and his gunpowder plot of 1605. It also sees bonfire societies holding up 17 burning crosses to remember the 17 Protestants burned in the High Street in the 16th century. You will also find another memorial to the 17 Protestant martyrs, this time an obelisk, looking down over Lewes from Cliffe Hill, which was erected in 1901.

# THE ROUND HOUSE

⑩

## *The house Virginia Woolf bought but never lived in*

*Pipe Passage*
*Lewes, East Sussex*

Virginia Woolf and her husband, Leonard, are well known around Sussex for living in Monk's House at Rodmell in East Sussex. They lived here for 22 years and it is where she wrote most of her major works, including *Mrs Dalloway* and *To the Lighthouse*, in a writing lodge at the bottom of the garden.

It is perhaps less well known, however, that just before they bought Monk's House, they bought this bizarrely shaped house completely on a whim, but they never ended up living in it. It is affectionately known as "the Round House" for obvious reasons. It can be found hidden up an interesting twitten in Lewes called Pipe Passage – itself a curiosity, as the centre of what was once a flourishing pipe manufacturing business (see below for more details).

"We've bought a house in Lewes on the spur of the moment. It's the butt end of an old windmill so that all the rooms are either completely round or semi-circular", reads a quote from Virginia Woolf on a plaque at the front of the house.

The windmill was originally built in 1801 to help with the food crisis caused by the Napoleonic wars. In 1819, the owner at the time, William Smart, removed the smock (the weatherboard tower), the sails and the interior workings, and took them to a new site near the barracks, where Lewes Prison now stands. The remaining building was immediately converted into a house.

## NEARBY

### *Location of a lost pipe-making industry*

Pipe Passage is also the setting for Lewes's lost pipe-making industry, hence its name. If you are approaching from Lewes High Street, just up the steps and a little way along on your left, you will see a fenced-off patch of land. It doesn't look like much, but these are the ramshackle remains of a workshop thought to have been built in the 1830s, where clay pipes used for smoking tobacco were made.

Clay tobacco pipe-making began in around 1580, probably in London, and spread across the country, springing up in the main cities and towns, especially those with access to suitable clay. Over the next 250 years, almost every city and town and many villages had a clay pipe maker.

Also in this enclosure, in the arch to the right, you can see the remnants of the brick kiln used to fire the pipes. When the site was excavated in 1956, some 700 pipe bowls were found. Markers on the pipes revealed that five different makers used the kiln between 1832 and 1878. One of these was George Corner who had a tobacconist's and pipe shop in the 1860s at 153 High Street, which is now a terraced family home.

# LEWES RAILWAY LAND NATURE RESERVE

⑪

*A secret urban retreat on a former railway yard*

*Lewes, East Sussex*
*railwaylandproject.org*

Surrounded by the busy A26 and A27 on the fringes of Lewes town centre, the Lewes Railway Land Nature Reserve is a peaceful town nature reserve on the site of an old railway yard: until 1989, a railway line linking Lewes with Uckfield ran over the Ouse river floodplain.

In its heyday, this area was nicknamed the "bone yard", and would have seen around 10,000 wagons pass through it every week. When the tracks were dismantled, the area became a wasteland. After 25 years of neglect, the land was saved from development by a group of local residents who formed the Railway Land Wildlife Trust.

Today, it has been completely reclaimed by nature and is now a thriving local nature reserve, made up of four distinct wetland habitats, each one vital for supporting the area's wildlife including several rare species.

Plenty of paths criss-cross the reserve making it easy to explore. A nice way to approach it is from an entrance at the end of Railway Lane off Cliffe High Street on the fringes of the town. Walk through a gate and you emerge into a quiet woodland, a million miles from the noise of the town.

This area once formed part of the Victorian Leighside Estate, over which the railway line ran on a now-demolished brick viaduct. The area has been interspersed with large Railway Poplars and a few more exotic specimen trees, including a Holm Oak and Swamp Cypress. It is also where you will find a restored duck pond filled with newts and fish.

The path then follows the old railway line further into the reserve – you will be able to spot the old sleepers in the ground – eventually emerging onto the flood plain grassland area backed by the town's well-recognised chalky cliffs.

It is a magical walk along the paths, up and over the bridge, around the meandering boardwalk, and the watery ditches. It is so peaceful you can hardly believe you are just moments away from the busy town, and the train to London.

A highlight is perhaps the swirling reed bed (pictured) – called "Heart of Reeds" – which is nice to look at from up on the little viewing platform nearby, and often attracts the singing reed warbler in summer.

All these habitats are irrigated by the Winterbourne stream which is fed by water filtered from the surrounding downland hills and only runs when it has been raining. In winter, the stream regularly overflows and fills these habitats with fresh water, keeping them in top condition. It then flows through the middle of the reserve and under giant tidal sluice gates into the Ouse.

# REMINDERS OF THE LEWES AVALANCHE

⑫

## *The white dress of a two-year-old girl, a pub name, a plaque ...*

*The Snowdrop Inn: 119 South Street, Lewes*
*Tablet: north wall of the South Malling church on Church Lane, Lewes*
*White dress: Anne of Cleves House Museum, 52 Southover High Street, Lewes*

The deadliest avalanche in British history is said to have taken place not in the mountains of Scotland or Wales as you might have expected, but in the county town of Lewes in East Sussex, where you will find several reminders of the event.

Today, a popular local pub in the town called the Snowdrop Inn stands on the site of this long forgotten and little-known deadly occurrence, known as the Lewes avalanche. The pub is thought to have been named in commemoration of the disaster, although some locals prefer to believe it is called after the snowdrop flowers planted on the victims' graves.

The pub was built in 1840 where a row of workers' cottages known as Boulder Row once stood. At the time of the avalanche, this was a poor part of the town, where entire families often shared single rooms.

During the winter of 1836, Britain suffered some of its worst weather ever recorded, with freezing temperatures, heavy snow and gale force winds. On Christmas Eve, a huge storm blew up over southern England and produced blizzards and massive snow drifts.

A large overhang of snow, known as a cornice, had started building up on the cliffs above the town, directly above Boulder Row. When it finally collapsed, it produced an enormous avalanche apparently heard across the whole town.

The avalanche killed seven people living in the cottages. The *Sussex Weekly Advertiser* at the time reported: "The mass appeared to strike the houses first at the base, heaving them upwards, and then breaking over them like a gigantic wave. There was nothing but a mound of pure white."

Those who died were too poor to afford individual funerals and were buried in an unmarked communal grave at South Malling Church just outside Lewes. Meanwhile, a fund was set up to provide financial aid to the survivors and bereaved families. One of those rescued from the avalanche was a two-year-old girl called Fanny Boakes.

The white dress she wore at the time can be seen on display at the Anne of Cleves House Museum in Lewes, along with a contemporary painting of the tragedy.

The avalanche is also marked by a simple memorial tablet which can be found on the north wall of South Malling church on Church Lane. John Harvard, of Harvard University fame, also married his wife, Ann Sadler here in 1636.

# GLYNDEBOURNE OPERA HOUSE BACKSTAGE TOURS ⑬

*Behind the scenes of a world-famous opera house*

*Glyndebourne Opera House*
*New Road, Lewes, East Sussex, BN8 5UU*
*01273 812321*
*glyndebourne.com/tickets-and-whats-on/events/2017/backstage-tours/*
*Open for tours every autumn and winter after the summer festival season*

Despite Glyndebourne Opera House's huge visitor numbers, few take advantage of – or even know about – the eye-opening 90-minute backstage tours that take place after the festival has finished.

These give inquisitive opera lovers a chance to understand Glyndebourne's history, go behind the scenes, discover where the action happens and find out the sheer magnitude of what is involved in staging world-renowned operatic performances.

Tours start with a brief introduction to the opera house in the organ room where the opera house was established. Visitors are then whisked around the grounds into the vast purpose-built 1,200-seat opera house, a £30 million building designed by Hopkins Architects and completed in 1993. You then go behind the scenes, through the warren of backstage corridors, along walkways over the stage, in and out of all kinds of rooms, such as the fly tower, the foyers, the green room, rehearsal studios and offices.

It is fun – or terrifying depending on how you look at it – to stand on the stage facing the audience seats, and get an idea of what it might feel like to be a performer in a production at Glyndebourne.

A detour backstage into the dressing rooms offers a reality check. They are all the same size no matter how famous the opera singer: there is no star hierarchy at Glyndebourne.

Arguably, a highlight of a backstage tour is the chance to snoop around the new state-of-the-art production hub. Built in 2018, it is where all the props, wigs and costume departments are located. This offers a close look at the costumes and wigs being made, and the levels of painstaking attention to detail and organisation involved.

After the tour, it is nice to reflect on all of this on a walk around the gardens, where you can admire the large-scale sculptures on display, and spot the curious Glyndebourne pugs (see p. 38).

The first-ever six-week festival season at Glyndebourne Opera House took place on 28 May 1934. The culmination of hard work by its founders, John Christie and his performer wife, Audrey Mildmay, it opened with a performance of Mozart's *The Marriage of Figaro* to an audience of 300 people.
Today, Glyndebourne hosts audiences of over 150,000 people a year during the summer season which runs from May to August, and also on its autumn tour, when its operas are staged at various venues around the country from October to December.

# GLYNDEBOURNE PUGS

(14)

*An ode to the opera house's founding family's love of dogs*

*The Mary Christie Rose Garden*
*Glyndebourne Opera House, New Road, Lewes, East Sussex, BN8 5UU*
*01273 812321*
*glyndebourne.com*
*Open to visitors of the Glyndebourne Festival which runs each year from May to August*

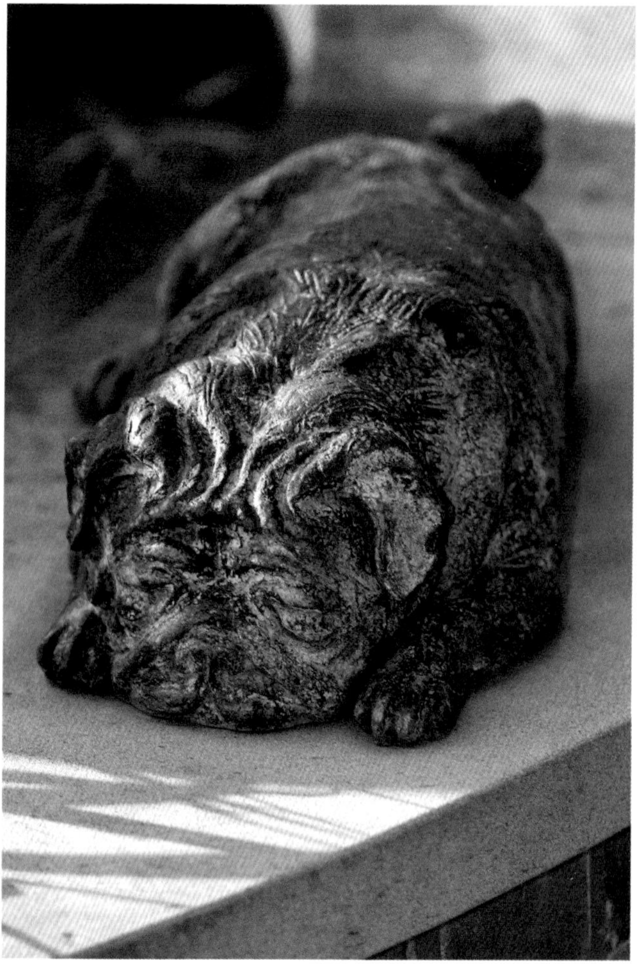

A large part of what makes seeing a performance at the world-famous Glyndebourne Opera House in East Sussex special, is the chance to explore the grounds and gardens, which are not otherwise open to the public.

With their sweeping views over the South Downs, they play a large part in the Glyndebourne Festival experience in that they become the magical setting for the famous Glyndebourne picnic, which ticketholders can enjoy during the 90-minute interval.

Each garden has its own unique style and curious features to discover.

The tranquil Figaro Garden is home to a Henry Moore sculpture – *Draped Reclining Woman* – and benches that overlook a reflecting pool. Exotic plants fill the sunken Bourne Garden, while the dizzying scent of wildflowers drifts through the Urn Garden.

The most bizarre discoveries, however, are sculptures of a pug dog lazing about in the Mary Christie Rose Garden – one playing in the roses, and another relaxing by the water. There is also another similar pug sculpture in the Organ Room.

The rose garden is the newest addition to the Glyndebourne landscape. It opened in 2015 when the opera house and grounds were remodelled. It was created as a tribute to Lady Christie, to honour her contribution and creative input into the Glyndebourne landscape.

The sculptures were added to celebrate the Christie family's love of pugs: there have been pugs in the family since the 1870s. Modelled on Lady Christie's beloved pet pug Fred, they were created by Rose Beale, a sculptor and also a senior props maker at Glyndebourne, who was specially commissioned to make them.

This involved carrying out a few "sittings" with Fred, who settled into poses similar to those captured in the final sculptures. They were originally made of clay, but later cast in bronze to make them more robust and develop a shine and patina over time from people reaching out to touch the paws or ears.

As well as the pugs, the garden is home to 850 types of roses which burst into bloom from early spring until late autumn. These include *Rosa Glyndebourne*, Glyndebourne's signature plant which is a bespoke new variety created in 2012 by Harkness Roses, old-fashioned shrub roses such as *Louise Odier* and *Blanc Double de Coubert*, and modern hybrids such as *Munstead Wood* and *Princess Alexandra of Kent*.

# THE LAVENDER LINE

15

## *Reliving the golden age of train travel*

*Isfield Station*
*Isfield near Uckfield, East Sussex, TN22 5XB*
*01825 750515*
*lavender-line.co.uk*
*Weekends 11am–4pm*

Isfield Station, which originally opened in 1858 to serve rural customers on the busy Brighton to Uckfield route, is the setting for the Lavender Line, a heritage railway which makes a 3.2-km round trip through the Sussex countryside to a station called Worth Holt in the hamlet of Little Horsted.

The original line closed in 1968 as part of the Government-initiated *Beeching Report* which saw a third of Britain's rail network axed. Today, Isfield Station has been completely restored and is now staffed entirely by volunteers who operate a number of different diesel and steam trains when it opens each weekend. In the name of authenticity, even uniformed guards are on board to hole-punch your old-style tickets and sound the whistle.

Inside the Grade-II listed signal box, which doubles up as a museum, you feel like you have stepped back in time to a golden age of train travel. The original signalling equipment is on display alongside cabinets filled with old photos and other nostalgic ephemera telling the story of the railway. As you browse, old recordings of whistles blowing and steam trains chugging away play in the background.

Meanwhile, a replica of the railway's original waiting room is the setting for a gift shop selling railway-related memorabilia. The fixtures of the original waiting room were removed in the early 1970s and relocated to the nationally popular Bluebell Railway as part of their model railway centre.

Riley's Miniature Railway is the most recent addition to the Lavender Line experience. It was built to raise money to buy equipment for St Thomas's Hospital in London to help children born with heart difficulties. There is also a children's playground and picnic area. The old original Victorian waiting room has been turned into an eatery called Cinders Café, complete with a beautifully restored original fireplace (see p. xxx).

## *A line not named after a local lavender field ...*

Contrary to what might be assumed, the Lavender Line heritage railway at Isfield Station is not named after a local lavender field, or anything lavender related in the vicinity. It is called after a local businessman, Mr A E Lavender. He owned a coal merchant business with headquarters in the nearby village of Ringmer but had an office at Isfield. You can still see his little wooden office building next to the cattle dock crane and model railway ticket office. This allowed nearby deliveries to be made straight from the railway yard.

# BOW BELLS MILESTONES

⑯

## *Originally used to mark the distance to Bow Bells Church in the City of London*

*At various points along the A22 and the A26*

At various points along the A22 and the A26 in Sussex is a series of white concrete markers which most people drive or walk past without noticing. An example that is easy to find is outside the British Heart Foundation shop on East Grinstead high street.

These are known as Bow Bells Milestones: local distance markers installed a mile apart along the old London to Eastbourne coaching roads. They were originally used to mark the distance to Bow Bells Church in the City of London and are thought to form part of the longest and most visible sequence of milestones in the country.

Some of the milestones have a black dot at the top, followed by a number, and three black bells. Others are topped with a buckle representing the Pelham family, wealthy landowners who lived in the nearby village of Halland at the time and who financed a southern extension of the turnpike in the 1750s.

The markers were installed by what were called "turnpike trusts". These were groups set up by Acts of Parliament in the 17th century to raise money to build stretches of road by charging users a toll. Little booths known as tollhouses were set up at toll-collection points along the coaching roads. The name turnpike comes from the spiked barrier in place at the tollhouses.

Milestone markers were first installed voluntarily by the trusts but, from 1767, their installation became compulsory. This was not only to let travellers know their direction and distances, but also to help coaches stick to their schedules. The distances were also used to calculate postal charges before the uniform postal rate was introduced in 1840.

At the height of the turnpike era, there were 20,000 miles of roads in the country with milestones. From the 1840s, however, rail travel superseded roads and many of the turnpike trusts were wound up. In 1888, the new county councils were given responsibility for main roads, and rural district councils that for minor routes. As faster motorised transport developed, so the importance of the milestones waned.

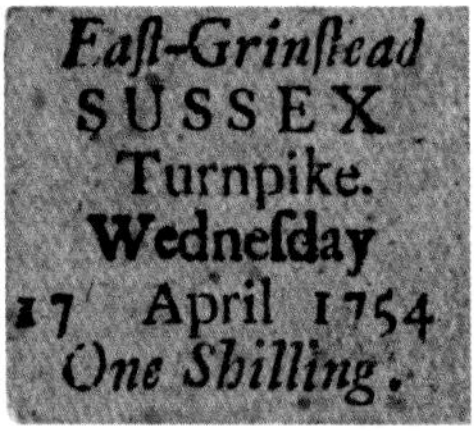


Tollhouses are separate curiosities in themselves. They were larger than you might imagine, with some of them resembling little cottages. They varied architecturally, but were typically one storey high with two or three rooms. You can see an original tollhouse from the village of Upper Beeding in East Sussex at The Weald and Downland Living Museum in West Sussex. See p. 100 for more information.

# FARLEYS HOUSE AND GALLERY ⑰

## *Where Picasso once came to tea*

*Muddles Green, Chiddingly, East Sussex, BN8 6HW*
*01825 872856*
*farleyshouseandgallery.co.uk*
*Tours every Thursday and Sunday, 10.30am–3.30pm, April to October*

After the Second World War, it was growing vegetables and cooking in her country kitchen which helped *Vogue* war photographer, Lee Miller – famed for the picture she took of herself in Hitler's bathtub – recover from her experiences, when she married Surrealist artist Roland Penrose and came to live at Farleys House in East Sussex.

The kitchen, like the rest of the house, remains almost in its original state, and is full of items which Miller and Penrose once used. In this case, kitchen utensils, cookbooks from Miller's vast collection, herbs, spices, gadgets of the time, and the odd great work of art, including a ceramic tile by their friend Pablo Picasso hanging just above the cooker (pictured).

"Conservators shudder at its position," says our guide on a morning tour of Farleys, "but the fact that it's hanging here highlights the couple's attitude to art, choosing to live with it in daily life".

Miller and Penrose lived at Farleys House for 35 years, during which time they built up a vast collection of contemporary art treasures, many created by their artist friends. These included Pablo Picasso, Man Ray, Max Ernst, Paul Éluard and Joan Miró. All of them are known to have visited Farleys at some point, which led to its reputation as the "house of the Surrealists".

Today, the Penrose family manages the house and collection as a privately run photographic archive and museum, including a sculpture garden and gallery, which you can visit on a guided tour every Sunday between April and October.

The dining room at Farleys, painted in Farmer's Weekly yellow, contains a collection of works of art designed to commemorate Roland Penrose: "a stoic and reserved character by nature who used art as a conduit for expressing his emotions", says our guide, who shows us paintings that reflect the different stages of his life and the progression of his style.

A few other pieces from Miller and Penrose's collection also decorate this room, including another Picasso and some pottery by local artist, Joyce Reeve – the couple loved to support local artisans. But it is Roland's Cubist-style mural decorating the fireplace that is most striking. Painted in 1950, a year after moving to Farleys, it depicts the legend of the Long Man of Wilmington (see p. 52) – a chalk figure on the South Downs – as a sun god, together with the planets, the moon and two cornucopia figures.

Lee's light-filled study with its views across the South Downs is perhaps the most architecturally spectacular room in the house. It was built in the 1960s for her to work in, and to house her vast collection of cookbooks – she had over 6,000 – many of which have been sold now. Today, it is home to books featuring the couple's work, as well as some original pieces of furniture, trinkets and a beautiful chest given to Lee by her father, inscribed with her name.

> The Penrose family also host a fun summer event known as the Surrealist Picnic every August (see p. 46).

# SURREALIST PICNIC

(18)

## *An eccentric summer garden party*

*Farleys House and Gallery*
*Muddles Green, Chiddingly, East Sussex, BN8 6HW*
*01825 872856*
*farleyshouseandgallery.co.uk/event/surrealist-picnic/*
*Every August bank holiday Sunday, 4pm–8pm*

Farleys House and Gallery sits in the pretty village of Muddles Green. It was once the country home of the Surrealist movement artist Roland Penrose and his wife, *Vogue* war photographer, Lee Miller. When they moved here in 1949, they began filling it with art created by locals and friends, including Pablo Picasso, Man Ray, Max Ernst, Paul Éluard and Joan Miró – all of whom were known to have visited Farleys at some point. This led to its nickname as the "house of the Surrealists", and you can learn more about its heritage on a tour (see p. 44).

Farleys also celebrates its Surrealist heritage with an annual themed summer garden party, known as the "Surrealist picnic". This takes place in the sculpture garden on the Sunday of the August bank holiday weekend, no matter what the weather.

This flamboyant gathering offers fans of the avant-garde Surrealist movement the chance to live out their creative fantasies, such as dressing up in "surreal" costumes and feasting on a "surreal" picnic. Pink cauliflower and blue pasta salad, a one-thousand-year-old egg, or a Casanova cocktail, anyone?

If you are yet to hone your Surrealist cooking skills, themed snacks are available during the event. These include cakes and ice lollies made from Lee Miller's recipes by local producers and cooks, such as Seven Sisters Spices.

This dreamlike summery soiree plays out against a backdrop of live jazz and alongside some bizarre dance performances. Previous years' line-ups include music from local bands The Hot Club of Jevington and Jonathan Bailey's Quartet, and performances by Found Dances and Sonia Sonalisa.

## *Get surreal ...*

The celebration of Farleys' Surrealist heritage does not stop at tours or summer garden parties. Various Surrealist-themed creative workshops are held at the house throughout the year. These include a one-day photography workshop in which beginners are shown how to develop a Surrealist eye in the style of Lee Miller, and cookery workshops which involve recreating Lee's Surrealist recipes in her kitchen using produce and herbs from the garden at Farleys House. For more information, see : farleyshouseandgallery.co.uk/workshops

## *Surrealism elsewhere in Sussex*

Roland Penrose and Lee Miller were not the only fans of the avant-garde to live in Sussex. The late owner of West Dean Gardens in West Sussex, Edward James, also made a significant contribution to the movement. See p.96 and p.98 for more details.

# DUNCAN GRANT'S STUDIO

(19)

## *As he left it before he died*

*Charleston,*
*Firle, East Sussex, BN8 6LL*
*01323 811626*
*charleston.org.uk*
*Daily house tours from March to October, 11.30pm–5pm*

Contrary to the perception that the Bloomsbury Group was predominantly literary, there is a wealth of visual art produced by its three chief painters: Vanessa Bell, Duncan Grant and Roger Fry. Their work occupies a significant place among the new movements in British art of the early 20th century, much of it created in the studio of their Sussex home, which you can see at the end of a tour of Charleston house.

In 1916, on Virginia Woolf's recommendation, the painters Vanessa Bell and Duncan Grant, his friend and lover David Garnett, and Vanessa Bell's two sons (Julian aged eight and Quentin aged six) along with Henry the dog, moved to Charleston, an ordinary farmhouse in East Sussex. Dating from the late 16th century and altered in the 19th century, it had previously been used as a boarding house. It was to be occupied and brought to life by the family and their friends for the next 64 years.

When the artists first came to Charleston, they painted in the house or in an old unheated army hut outside. Called "Les Misérables", it was set up beyond the walled garden as a studio. In 1925, a proper studio was built onto the house, on the site of a former chicken run. The artists shared this until 1939 when Vanessa Bell, needing privacy, decided to turn an attic bedroom into a north-facing studio.

Walking into the studio you are immediately captivated by the space, and might well feel an enormous urge to be creative. Light streams down into the room from overhead, and the walls are painted in neutral tones, creating a simple background for paintings. There are ephemera everywhere. The mantelpiece and surround, covered in postcards, ornaments and other items, is sure to engage your attention for a good five minutes.

One of the most interesting pieces in the room is an early 19th-century Dutch walnut cabinet. This is one of a pair which were once in the house of the novelist WM Thackeray, author of *Vanity Fair*. Thackeray's younger daughter, Minny, was the first wife of Vanessa Bell's father, Leslie Stephen.

The cabinet contains a collection of glass and ceramics, some decorated by the Charleston artists, including four Famous Women plates from a service decorated for the British art historian, Kenneth Clark, in 1932.

Duncan Grant continued to work in the original studio until shortly before he died in 1978. The room we see on the tour looks very much as he left it, still containing many of the materials he used for painting.

# THE BLOOMSBURY MURALS

20

## *A hidden heavenly sight*

*St Michael and All Angels Church*
*Berwick, Polegate, East Sussex, BN26 6SR*
*berwickchurch.org.uk*
*Daily from 9am–6pm, or dusk if earlier*

The Sussex countryside is littered with pretty churches, but there is one in a corner of East Sussex which is unique because of its interior, decorated by the famous Bloomsbury group artists, Duncan Grant, Vanessa Bell – Virginia Woolf's sister – and Quentin Bell, who had their rural headquarters at the nearby Charleston farmhouse (see p. 48).

Stepping inside the darkened church, the colourful murals are cast in shadow, so are not immediately obvious until you press a switch on the wall by the leaflet-covered table. The lights gradually illuminate the murals, which makes for a heavenly sight when fully lit.

The murals were commissioned by Bishop Bell of Chichester in 1941. He wanted to revive the tradition of painting murals in churches, a practice that was common before the Reformation. The ones inside St Michael and All Angels Church depict local people, sometimes wearing period clothes, acting out biblical scenes. The artists' choice of theme and subject matter is said to reflect their thoughts on the intimacy of home and personal relationships, and the beauty of the Sussex Downs landscape.

Duncan Grant was lead artist on the project, and it is thought his designs were heavily influenced by his travels around Europe, which he had undertaken with Vanessa Bell. Particular influences include the Byzantine mosaics at Ravenna, a city in northern Italy known as the "city of mosaics", frescoes by the early Renaissance Italian artist Piero della Francesca, and works by the 18th-century French painter Jean-Baptiste-Siméon Chardin, portraying scenes of everyday life, such as ordinary people at work or leisure. Grant also studied the work of the Impressionist painters and was later greatly influenced by the Post-Impressionists, such as Cézanne, Matisse and others.

> The Bloomsbury Group of artists were pioneers of their time in British art and literature. They openly rejected the traditional Victorian ideals they had been brought up with. They were as well known for their art and literary talents as their unconventional lifestyles and liberal attitudes, which famously included complicated love triangles, extravagant hoaxes and their support for gay rights.

### *Lost Saxon art*

A much older set of murals exists inside St John the Baptist church in Clayton, East Sussex. They date back to the 11th century and until recently no one knew they were there. Find the church at Underhill Lane, Clayton, East Sussex BN6 9PJ.

# LONG MAN OF WILMINGTON

㉑

## *The mysterious guardian of the South Downs*

*South Downs Way, Wilmington, Eastbourne, East Sussex, BN26 5SW*

Known as the Long Man of Wilmington, or the Wilmington Giant, the enormous chalk carving of a man wielding two spears, cut into the steep slope of Windover Hill facing north, is one of around 50 landscape features in Great Britain known as "hill figures".

It is also one of two which depict the human figure: the other is the Cerne Abbas Giant in Dorset.

At almost 69 metres high, the Long Man of Wilmington is also one of the largest representations of a human figure to be found anywhere in the world.

Much of southern England is made up of chalk covered in a thin layer of soil and vegetation. For centuries, people have been scratching away at this top section to create these enormous chalk carvings.

Information on its origins and what it is thought to represent remains vague. Some believe it was created by monks from nearby Wilmington Priory between the 11th and 15th centuries. Other theories suggest it was created during the Iron Age, or dates back to Roman times, a similar figure having been noted on 4th-century coins and Anglo-Saxon ornaments. Recent archaeological work strongly suggests that the figure was created during the 16th or 17th century, although no one really knows for sure.

Until the 19th century, you could only see the Long Man in certain light conditions and after a light fall of snow, but in 1874, it was marked out in yellow bricks to make seeing it much easier. It is claimed that during this restoration the feet were incorrectly positioned, but despite popular local legend, there is no evidence, historical or archaeological, to suggest that this is true.

During the Second World War, the figure was painted green to prevent enemy aviators using it as a landmark. It was restored in 1969: the bricks were replaced with pre-cast concrete blocks that are now regularly painted to ensure that the Long Man remains visible from many miles away.

## NEARBY

### *Long Man Brewery Tours*

*Long Man Brewery, Church Farm, Litlington, East Sussex, BN26 5RA*
*01323 871850*
*longmanbrewery.co.uk*

Taking its name from the Long Man of Wilmington, the *Long Man Brewery* offers tours and tastings of its naturally produced beer at its facility in the pretty village of Litlington, at the foot of Windover Hill in the South Downs.

# SHERLOCK HOLMES' FICTIONAL HOME ㉒

## *Retirement home of a London super sleuth*

*The Green*
*East Dean, Eastbourne, East Sussex, BN20 0BT*
*Open to view from the outside only*

The village of East Dean near Eastbourne is one of those perfect chocolate-box Sussex villages, with pretty cottages, a pub, and some cafes surrounding a green, all backed by the rolling South Downs. It makes the perfect detour on the way to or from fossil hunting (see p. 58) or a visit to The Cable Hut (see p. 56). It is also a destination in itself, with literary connections.

Opposite New House Farm on the green, there is one particularly attractive cottage which stands out, not only for its appearance, but also for the blue plaque on the front. The plaque marks the fictional retirement home of Sherlock Holmes, Sir Arthur Conan Doyle's, proficient consulting private detective – who it is thought retired to the countryside around Eastbourne to become a beekeeper.

Holmes obsessives and experts have long maintained that the detective moved to the South Downs from the heady heights of 221b Baker Street in London. The exact location is unknown, Conan Doyle having only offered vague hints throughout his stories about the detective. The site was chosen after years spent studying clues in the stories and advice from the Sherlock Holmes Society.

For example, Sussex is mentioned as the location a couple of times. In *His Last Bow*, Dr Watson tells us Holmes "retired to a small farm upon the Downs, five miles from Eastbourne". In *The Adventure of the Lion's Mane*, Holmes tells us that his "lonely" home has commanding views over the English Channel at a point where "the coastline is entirely of chalk cliffs which can only be descended by a single, long tortuous path, which is steep and slippery".

One expert thinks it is clear that Sherlock Holmes retired to a building located between Eastbourne and Seaford (there are no cliffs east of Eastbourne). The location has to be inland as you cannot keep bees on a cliff edge, so five miles would make the location East Dean or maybe Friston.

It is also known that beekeeping requires a sheltered spot, a fact which has ruled out a number of potential retirement spots in the area. East Dean though, is sheltered from the coastal gales, and therefore still a genuine contender.

Also, Conan Doyle knew the area well, having been born in Crowborough. He was said to have been a regular visitor to the Eastbourne area during his later years.

> A bronze statue of the detective's creator, Sir Arthur Conan Doyle, can be found at Cloak's Corner in Crowborough, where he lived for over 20 years and where he created the world-famous detective.

# THE CABLE HUT

23

*A strange building which reflects the area's early communications heritage*

*1-2 Coastguard Cottages, Cuckmere Haven, Seaford, East Sussex, BN25 4AR*
*heritageopendays.org.uk*
*Open during Heritage Open weekends*

Cuckmere Haven lies in the Cuckmere Valley at the point where the South Downs meet the sea. Its dramatic landscape and characteristic chalk cliffs attract tourists from all over the world. It has also become a favourite subject for artists, photographers, filmmakers, writers and lately, Instagrammers.

Of the thousands of visitors walking along the coastal footpath for a view of the chalky Seven Sisters cliffs, most overlook an unusual flat-roofed building hidden behind a black fence, not far from the Coastguard Cottages near an overlooked beach called Hope Gap.

This is what is known as the Cable Hut, a curious structure which reflects the area's early communications heritage. Today, it is privately owned by the Ann family. They use it to house their bathing, fishing and boating equipment and as a base from which to enjoy days on the beach together. They occasionally open it up to the public during Heritage Open Days, to help publicise the local "Cuckmere Haven SOS" campaign. This aims to raise money to improve sea defences and protect the chalky cliffs around Cuckmere Haven from erosion.

It is also the perfect opportunity for curious visitors to have a peek inside at its pretty interior, complete with a "picture window" which perfectly frames the chalky cliffs of the Seven Sisters.

The hut was built by the Anglo-American Telegraph Company as a cable station from which to operate telegraph lines running under the sea to France. The American communications company Western Union took over the operation at some point and, by 1918, there were three telegraph lines in operation: one running from Cuckmere Haven to Le Havre in Normandy and two more running to Cap d'Antifer, also in Normandy.

Like so many other buildings in the area, the hut was requisitioned by the military in the Second World War.

In 1940, the lines were cut and the hut converted into a "pill box", a type of guard post. This was done by lowering the roof and inserting gun slits, through which weapons could be fired. By the end of the war, it had been almost entirely demolished by gunfire.

In 1947, the cable station was moved to a nearby parcel of land obtained in a deal made with Captain Douglas Ann, the father of the hut's present owner. He agreed to swap the site of his tea house at Exceat bridge just up the river, for the ruined building's site by the sea. Captain Ann restored the hut as a place for storing his fishing gear, appealing against local council plans to tear it down and reinstate it as a ruin.

# SECRET SPOTS FOR FOSSIL HUNTING

(24)

*Tracing signs of prehistoric life*

*Peacehaven and Hope Gap, East Sussex*

There is something other-worldly about the stretch of the East Sussex coast from Saltdean near Brighton to Birling Gap near Eastbourne. Generally speaking, though, most visitors overlook so much of it in favour of the famous Seven Sisters Country Park.

This area encompasses Cuckmere Haven with its meandering estuary, Birling Gap home to the famed Belle Tout Lighthouse, and the iconic film set of Beachy Head – all well-known on this section of coast known as the Sussex Heritage Coast.

With its undulating coastal path and white cliff views – particularly attractive bathed in pink light at dusk – it attracts people in droves from around the world.

If you can resist its lure, however, the beach at Peacehaven – although not officially part of the Sussex Heritage coast and not quite so stunning – offers the same dramatic landscape, complete with white cliffs. It is also the setting for an alternative, off-beat activity which will help you learn more about the landscape: fossil hunting.

There are some incredible fossils to be found here, including giant *Parapuzosia* ammonites, measuring over 6 feet across in some cases. Despite their size, the ammonites are not immediately apparent to passers-by, so they are best seen at low tide, when it is also likely you will have the place all to yourself. They can be found in both directions from the access point at Peacehaven steps. A variety of other fossils can also be found on the foreshore, in particular echinoids, sponges and bivalves. If you are not sure, previous fossil hunters have written instructions on the sea wall on where to find them.

If, however, you cannot resist the lure of the Seven Sisters Country Park, and would like to hunt for fossils there, head to a secluded beach called Hope Gap. This is another secluded fossil hunting spot, not far from the Coastguard Cottages and the curious Cable Hut (see p. 56). Just west of these buildings, you will notice a set of steep steps which lead down to it. Most people seem to either wander on past the steps, or venture down, but just take a quick look and then come back up, which means it is never crowded.

Fossils can be found in either direction on this beach, although the best exposures are found towards Seaford in the northwest. The most productive (and safest) place to search for fossils is on the foreshore at low tide. Chalk boulders and flint nodules are scattered along the entire section, providing a constant supply of fossils.

Common finds include echinoids, brachiopods, bivalves and sponges; while less common are crustacean burrows lined with fish scales and starfish remains, among others.

The reason that this area is good for fossil hunting is that the chalk cliffs and foreshore at Seaford Head contain relics of a complex marine environment that dates from what is known as the Late Cretaceous epoch, around 86 million years ago.

# TIDE MILLS ABANDONED VILLAGE

25

## *A forgotten village by the sea*

*Near Newhaven, Seaford, East Sussex, BN25 2TW*

Tucked away between Newhaven in East Sussex and The Buckle at Seaford are the ghostly remains of the lost village of Tide Mills.

There are two ways to find it: take the single-track Mill Drove signposted "Tide Mills" off the main road to and from Newhaven, then cross the railway at Bishopstone Beach Halt. Alternatively, you could also reach it on a stroll along the beach to the east of Newhaven Harbour.

Approaching from the old Bishopstone Beach Halt station is an atmospheric walk down to the sea as you wander around the stone walls, along concrete tracks, past all the old foundations of lost buildings. As you are walking, it is hard not to imagine what kind of life people had in this isolated village by the sea, and who exactly lived here.

Tide Mills was established in 1761 when the Duke of Newcastle gave three West Sussex corn merchants permission to build a dam and mill where the river Ouse once met the sea. The mill was driven by the power of the tide, and ground corn into flour for transport across southern England, and to meet increasing demand in London. By the mid 1800s, it was a thriving village where mill workers lived, and continued to grow and develop as the mill prospered.

Although the mill closed in 1883, people carried on living in the village. At the time of the census in 1911, 15 households were recorded at Tide Mills, making a total population of 75.

It was also used as a sea plane base during the First World War to help combat the threat from submarines. In the 1920s, it was used as the location for a hospital for sick children and as racing stables belonging to a wealthy local gentleman called Captain David Dale. By 1941, the village had been evacuated and was used for military training during the Second World War. What remained of the settlement after the war was then removed.

Information boards set up around the remains help us understand it better and there is also a useful map showing the village as it was in the late 1800s. The site is constantly being archaeologically surveyed with new information expected to be added in the future.

## *A good spot for birdwatching*

As well as the setting for some 'urban' exploration, Tide Mills has become a good spot for birdwatching due to its location next to the sea and the Ouse Valley Nature Reserve. Species such as purple sandpiper and ringed plover have been spotted at the site. Other wildlife to look out for here include the long tailed blue butterfly (a rare migrant which has been visiting the site for the last few years), grass snakes and other reptiles.

# THE RAMPION TELESCOPES

(26)

*Windows on a mysterious world out at sea*

*West Sussex: Lancing, Worthing, Shoreham-by-Sea*
*East Sussex: Rottingdean, Seaford, Newhaven*
*rampionoffshorewindfarm.com/wind-farm/map*

Some like it and are fascinated by it, while others deeply despise it. Either way, the Rampion Offshore Wind Farm – an eerie, controversial permanent fixture on the Sussex horizon – is here to stay. The project and its progress sparked as much curiosity as it did local resistance, which led to the initiation of a project to install six telescopes along the Sussex coast to encourage long-term interest in the wind farm once fully operational.

Its construction began in 2016, at which point strange dark shapes began appearing in the distance. Pillars emerged from the sea, while the rigs that did the actual building work seemed to hover magically above the water, shifting positions every few days.

The idea for the telescopes came from pupils at Globe Primary School in Lancing who approached Lancing Council. Rampion loved the idea so much it partnered with three more local councils in the area. The first four telescopes were installed in Lancing, Newhaven, Rottingdean and Shoreham. They were so popular that two more were added in Worthing and Seaford.

In West Sussex, the telescopes can be found in Denton Gardens in Worthing, Beech Green in Lancing, and the west end of Shoreham Beach Boardwalk (see p. 210) in Shoreham-by-Sea. In East Sussex, you will find them at the Quarterdeck at the south end of Lower High Street in Rottingdean, on Seaford promenade, close to Seaford Museum, and at the foot of the Coastwatch Tower on Castle Hill in Newhaven (pictured). You can also check their locations on the map at the website opposite.

The Rampion Wind Farm spans 72 square kilometres – only slightly smaller than the one at Brighton and Hove, which measures 87.5 square kilometres. Rampion claims that the wind farm will generate enough green electricity to power the equivalent of around 350,000 UK homes. This is equal to almost half the homes in Sussex.

## *Boat trips to the wind farm*

Visitors can also learn more about the Rampion Offshore Wind Farm story, and wind energy in general, at the new Rampion visitors' centre on Brighton seafront, just east of the British Airways i360 Viewing Tower. However, if reading about it and peering at it through telescopes is just not enough to satisfy your interest, a number of local charter boat operators offer boat trips to the wind farm, for the chance to weave in and around the giant turbines, and the ultimate close-up view. For more information, visit rampionoffshore.com/about/visiting-rampion/charter-boat-operators/

N
A325
A3
A287
A286
A283
A281
SURREY
Bordon
HAMPSHIRE
A3
Haslemere
A325
Liphook
B2133
Loxwood
Ifold
Northchapel
Fernhurst
A3
Milland
A286
A283
Kirdford
A272
A272
Lodsworth
A272
Midhurst
A272
Petworth
South
Harting
B2146
Rother
A283
Arun
Fittleworth
A286
B2138
A285
B2146
B2141
Singleton
East Dean
Bury
A286
A29
A284
A285
Funtington
Fontwell
A27
A27
Arundel
A27
Southbourne
A27
B2233
West
Barnham
A259
Chichester
A29
Yapton
A259
A259
Littlehampton
Thorney
Island
A286
B2145
B2186
B2259
Bogna Regis
Wittering
Sussex Bay
Selsey
Selsey
Bill
0
5
10 km
1
2
3
4
5
6
7
8
9
10
11
12
13
14
15
16
17
18
19
20
21
22
23
24

# *Chichester to Petworth*

# THORNEY ISLAND CIRCULAR WALK

①

## *A remote experience*

*Thorney Island, Chichester Harbour, West Sussex*
*Access is available at all times but you must follow the path*
*Find more information and a trail map here:*
*assets.publishing.service.gov.uk/government/uploads/system/uploads/attachment_data/file/27464/ThorneyIsland.pdf*

Apart from the odd hiker or person doing a spot of fishing, it is unlikely that you will encounter another soul on this remote 11-km circular walk around Thorney Island, a peninsula of Chichester Harbour.

It is not technically an island either. Although it is separated from the mainland by a channel, Thorney Island (named after all the hawthorn bushes) and Pilsey Island have effectively been joined to the mainland since the reclamation of tidal mudflats in 1870.

It was first used by the Royal Air Force in 1935 and was a fighter station and base for Coastal Command during the Second World War. In 1984, it was taken over by the Army and it is now a home base for the Army.

This explains the hostile-looking gated security entrances at either end of the walk topped with razor wire and imposing CCTV cameras. You would be forgiven for thinking you had stepped onto a spy movie set. Don't let this harsh greeting put you off being here, though. It is simply a formality that the Military of Defence require details of all visitors entering – and leaving – their land, which you provide by pressing a buzzer on an intercom to the guardroom which controls the gate by remote control.

To enjoy Thorney Island, you must follow the coastal walking path around its perimeter, which offers breathtaking views across the mudflats all around – deviate from it into the barracks at your peril. It is possible to walk either way around the island, as both directions offer interesting and varied perspectives. The path is clearly waymarked around the island; the waymarker sign is a curlew.

There are various highlights dotted around the island. One is a little birdwatching hide at the tip of the peninsula, which is a nice place to stop for lunch, offering views of Pilsey Island, an RSPB bird sanctuary. Thorney Island has been Ministry of Defence land since 1938 and, as a result of the lack of intensive farming, has become a haven for wildlife. It has been designated a site of special scientific interest due to its saltwater reed beds. Bird species include brent geese, oystercatchers, lapwings, curlews, skylarks and shelduck. The tufty grasses and windswept sand of Pilsey are a favourite with ospreys stopping off on their way from Africa to Scotland and in the 1970s, it was apparently where the first egrets nested in Britain.

It is incredible to discover the beautiful deserted sandy beach which makes a nice summer escape from the crowds at West Witterings, and the atmospheric 11th-century church of St Nicholas which is occasionally open.

# RACTON MONUMENT

②

## *A hidden ruin*

*Stoughton*
*Chichester, West Sussex, PO18 9DU*

On the fringes of the Stansted Park Estate, just south of the Lordington Lavender field (see p. 70) is an abandoned architectural oddity, on a hill surrounded by trees, waiting to be discovered on a ramble around the area.

This 24-metre-high tower or folly is known as the Racton monument (or Racton ruin). To get to it, walk along a gated public bridle way off the Funtington Road, where you will see it emerge in a clearing about 200 metres up the track on the left.

The floors and much of the original flint facing have long since disappeared and its roof is caving in. Like most unprotected ruins, nature is fast taking over. Many of the holes, which presumably were once windows, are filled with ivy and trees, while a lot of the brickwork inside and out is covered in graffiti – additional features which only add to its eerie abandoned appeal.

Today, the beer cans strewn around inside and out and the graffiti are clues which suggest it is a secret setting for youthful escapism, even though it actually belongs to a private owner. According to local news reports, the owner did have planning permission to turn the monument into a dwelling, but the plans are yet to materialise.

It is said to have been built by the second Earl of Halifax. Like so many of these bizarre folly-type structures scattered around Britain, no one really knows why, although obviously plenty of rumours exist.

Some say it was used as a summerhouse to complement the Earl's nearby Stansted Estate, while others suggest he used it to look out for his merchant ships docking at the nearby port village of Emsworth. Another theory is that he wanted to watch for his son's return from an ill-fated voyage.

Designed by an architect called Theodosius Keene, son of Henry Keene, it was built between 1766 and 1775 with a triangular base and a round turret at each corner and is made out of bricks originally faced with flint.

With its eerie abandoned appearance and mysterious origins, it is no wonder it attracts rebellious teenagers and urban explorers. It is also reportedly haunted, and has become a regular hangout for people fascinated by the paranormal. Groups have carried out investigations and reported various ghostly activities at the site. Witnesses claim to have seen bricks thrown from above, heard ghostly shouts, and there is also a legend that the folly may have been used by smugglers.

# LORDINGTON LAVENDER WEEK ③

## *A magnificent little-known bloom*

*Lordington Lavender Farm*
*Farm Lane, Lordington, Chichester, West Sussex, PO18 9DX*
*07793 499327*
*lordingtonlavender.co.uk*
*Second week of July each year, 10am–4pm*

For seven days in the height of summer, a hidden corner of the South Downs near Chichester turns a heady haze of violet-blue when thousands of lavender plants burst into brilliant bloom.

A wander through the perfumed rows is a sight – and experience – to behold; one that transports us sensorially to the lavender fields of Provence in the south of France.

Lordington Lavender Farm was set up in 2002 by a local dairy farmer, Andrew Elms, and forms part of his family's 750-acre arable farm. He started growing lavender as a passion project having sold his 180-strong herd of dairy cows.

The lavender field consists of four acres filled with 26,500 plants of Maillette lavender, a French variety known for its high-quality oil, which the Lordington team harvests every year.

They originally used it to make oil but now have an entire range of products. The plants are harvested by machine then stored in an airtight trailer. Steam is then pumped in through the bottom of the trailer for six hours. It exits through a chimney into a condenser, where it evaporates, leaving the oil behind.

As well as the idyllic setting for a fragrant walk and a photography shoot, the rows of lavender blooms act as a natural haven for wildlife all year. At least 12 red listed species of birds, including skylarks and barn owls, have been found on the farm. Swarms of endangered bumble bees and dozens of species of butterfly have also been spotted here. The dense woody stems make perfect nests for field mice and voles, and hide hares and their leverets.

The lavender field was in fact created as an experimentation in diversification, and particularly as a way to encourage wildlife and birds, which is why it is grown without fertilisers and pesticides.

"I actually chose to grow lavender to help the endangered bumble bee," says Andrew. "I belong to the Guild of Conservation producers whose aim is to farm in harmony with nature and provide a wide range of habitats for the flora and fauna of the farm. It's been a success as the thousands of bees will testify," he adds.

"We also grow it with conservation of habitat and the environment very much in mind which is why we grow it without pesticides and fertilisers."

### *Secret nights on the lavender farm*

On select evenings during Lordington Lavender Week, the farm becomes the glorious setting for a sunset cocktail and barbecue. Visit lordingtonlavender.co.uk for more details.

# KINGLEY VALE NATURE RESERVE TRAIL ④

*An atmospheric walk through an ancient forest*

*South Downs National Park, Chichester, West Sussex*
*visitchichester.org/activity/kingley-vale-trail*
*From dawn to dusk*

Near the village of West Stoke close to Chichester is a unique nature reserve, home to Europe's largest yew forest.

It is worth the effort to find Kingley Vale, if only to walk through the yew groves and under the ancient canopy of twisted arching yew tree boughs. It is a humbling, transportive experience: you almost half expect to witness a druidic rite or medieval banquet, or to stumble on the *Game of Thrones* film set.

Considering most yew trees in Britain were cut down after the 14th century to make into longbows, those at Kingley Vale are remarkable for surviving.

No one knows exactly how old they are, although some are said to have celebrated their 2000th birthday. They are also intimidatingly gigantic – the oldest yew in the forest measures over five metres in girth.

A nice option is to start exploring from the small car park at the foot of the hill just west of the church at West Stoke. Through a gate, you follow a stony farm track north towards the woodland, eventually emerging into open countryside before you reach a crossroads, where an ancient bridleway crosses Stoke Down. The nature reserve is straight ahead, and the way-marked nature trail starts at the information hut.

The best of the oldest yews are on the right-hand side, about 20 really old, twisted veterans – including the Kingley Vale Great Yew – the Woodland Trust's "Tree of the Year" nominee 2019 (pictured).

The reserve is also the habitat for 11 different species of orchid, various birds and 39 of the 58 species of butterfly that breed in England. It is also home to one of the most important concentrations of well-preserved archaeological sites in southern England, including 14 Scheduled Monuments of which the Devil's Humps and Goosehill are the most prominent.

Towards the end of the trail is a giant rock up on a hill. It is known as the Arthur Tansley stone. This is a memorial to the man who started Natural England, the Government's advisory group for the natural environment in England. www.gov.uk/government/organisations/natural-england. The best place to ponder this incredible place is at the top of Bow Hill, with its jaw-dropping view over to Chichester Harbour and Thorney Island (see p. 66).

# PEREGRINE FALCONS OF CHICHESTER CATHEDRAL

5

## *Feathered squatters*

*Chichester Cathedral*
*The Royal Chantry, Cathedral Cloisters, Chichester, West Sussex, PO19 1PX*
*chichesterperegrines.co.uk*
*Open to view from the outside or up close on an open day*
*See above link for details*
*Cathedral open Monday to Saturday, 7.15am–6.30pm, Sunday 7.15am–5pm*

Every year in Chichester from around May to July, visitors to the cathedral can witness an incredible sight: adult and young peregrine falcons swooping in and out of their nest in the spire.

You can catch a glimpse looking up from the grounds, and baby peregrine falcons have also been spotted in the café gardens.

The first ever sighting of the nesting birds here was sometime in the mid-1990s, although it is thought they may have been nesting here unrecorded for hundreds of years before. They return each year to nest and raise their young.

These magnificent birds of prey can grow up to half a metre in length and have a wingspan of over one metre. They live for 15 to 18 years and are considered the fastest animals in the world, diving at speeds of just under 250mph to catch their prey. They are also incredibly agile and have even been observed flying upside down to catch food. Peregrine falcons were driven to near extinction in the UK due to the use of pesticides and active persecution. Today, the birds are protected by laws reinforced by European legislation known as the Nature Directives.

The birds live in the spire until the young have fledged; that is until they have been taught how to hunt and catch their food. Sometimes, a reluctant young falcon will hang around hoping for a free meal. They are usually chased off by the time the next nesting season comes around.

It is not known where all the offspring go when they have fledged, although it is thought that a few of them live in Brighton. Others have been seen in Cambridge, Canterbury and Norwich, and as far afield as Holland, France and Belgium.

Two local wildlife enthusiasts and photographers, Janet and David Shaw, have been monitoring the peregrine falcons at Chichester Cathedral each year since they found out they were there in 2001. They were so inspired by what they saw that they set up the Peregrine Project as a way of sharing their photos and news of the birds. Today, they run the project alongside the cathedral and Sussex Ornithological Society.

During the nesting season, they post news of the birds on their website and blog (chichesterperegrinesblog.co.uk), and most recently set up a webcam which streams live footage of the nesting birds into the cathedral café.

If you are keen to find out more about these fascinating birds, curious bird-spotters can take a closer look at them on one of several free open days set up by David and Janet. For more information, visit chichesterperegrinesblog.co.uk

# CASS SCULPTURE FOUNDATION COLLECTION ⑥

*Preserving the legacy of a lost and little-known sculpture park*

*Pallant House Gallery*
*8-9 North Pallant, Chichester, West Sussex, PO19 1TJ*
*01243 774557*
*pallant.org.uk*
*Call ahead of your visit to find the current display status*
*Archive to view by appointment only*

Up until it permanently closed in late 2019, the CASS Sculpture Foundation was one of Britain's most underrated sculpture parks: a little-known 26-acre, open-air art gallery nestled in woodland behind Goodwood racecourse.

Its legacy now lives on at Pallant House Gallery in Chichester, which acquired a significant part of the CASS collection. This includes some 40 maquettes, preparatory drawings and works on paper relating to contemporary British sculpture.

Highlights of the collection include two maquettes relating to large-scale works commissioned for the empty fourth plinth in Trafalgar Square in 1999: Rachel Whiteread's *Untitled Monument* and Bill Woodrow's *Regardless of History*. Further memorable pieces are Eduardo Paolozzi's *London to Paris* plaster maquette for a work commissioned by CASS in 2000 (one of the last he made before his death), a group of maquettes and drawings by Peter Randall Page inspired by natural form and pattern, and additional maquettes by Ralph Brown, Marc Quinn, Tony Cragg and William Tucker.

The selection also includes work by Helaine Blumenfeld, Cathy de Monchaux, Shirazeh Houshiary and Wendy Ramshaw, to enrich its representation of female artists.

A visit to the CASS Sculpture Foundation was a special experience, offering the chance to discover impressive large-scale art works spaciously set amid woodland and countryside on a self-guided trail through a forest. And of course, because all the sculptures in the park were for sale, no two visits were ever the same.

The foundation was opened in 1994 by art lovers Wilfred and Jeannette Cass, who pioneered a new way of commissioning art. They would fund up-and-coming artists to make pieces they had always dreamt of making but for which they did not have the financial resources. When pieces were sold, the artists and CASS would share the profits so new commissions could be taken on; each one a catalyst for new creative and professional opportunities.

CASS kick-started the careers of some of the UK's leading contemporary artists. These included Anthony Caro, Tony Cragg, Andy Goldsworthy (see p. 102), Mark Quinn, Gavin Turk, Rachel Whiteread, Eduardo Paolozzi and many others. Some of the works supported by CASS have also been exhibited and acquired by cultural institutions in the UK and abroad, including Peggy Guggenheim in Venice, Ekebergparken in Oslo, Tate Britain, the V&A, the Natural History Museum, the Science Museum, the Holland Park Festival in London, the State Hermitage in St Petersburg and the Museum of Contemporary Art in Tokyo.

# MARC CHAGALL WINDOW

⑦

## *Modernism meets ancient religion*

*Chichester Cathedral*
*The Royal Chantry, Cathedral Cloisters, Chichester, West Sussex, PO19 1PX*
*01243 782595*
*chichestercathedral.org*
*Monday to Saturday 7.15am–6.30pm, Sunday 7.15am–5pm*
*Admission free*

Generally speaking, stained glass windows within religious settings all tend to look the same, each depicting a biblical scene in a similarly traditional style. However, Chichester Cathedral is home to a window which stands out for its vibrant colour scheme and Modernist approach.

Set in the north-east corner next to the Chapel of St John the Baptist, the striking and colour-rich window is an interpretation of Psalm 150 by the Russian-French artist Marc Chagall, well-known for his brilliant use of colour and lively, imaginative decorative stained-glass art works which often combine elements of Cubism and Fauvism with his folkish style.

The window was commissioned by Walter Hussey, Dean of Chichester, who was inspired by windows which Chagall had created for the synagogue of the Hadassah Hospital in Jerusalem, and which were on show during a special exhibition at The Louvre in Paris in 1960.

The hospital windows and this one at Chichester Cathedral are the only glass pieces by Chagall which are predominantly created in red; his preferred colour was blue.

On close inspection, you can see all the musical instruments mentioned in the psalm: from the Jewish harp played by King David at the top, to the strings (bottom left) and the trumpet (bottom right). There is also a reference to literature: a creature on the extreme right (fourth section down) is holding a book, while two figures (centre left) hold aloft the seven-branched candlestick.

A number of animals and birds appear in the window, perhaps representing members of God's kingdom who join in the praise.

Marc Chagall grew up in the Jewish communities of Eastern Europe, in a world which was destroyed by the Nazis only to blossom afresh in the free air of the Western democracies. He drew his inspiration from Jewish religious life, especially the mystical Hasidic sects that flourished in his hometown of Vitebsk (Belarus).

The only other stained-glass work by Chagall in England can be found in All Saints Church near Tunbridge Wells in Kent. It consists of a collection of 12 windows in which angels and asses, saints and butterflies collide in a kaleidoscope of colour.

## *Another curiosity of Chichester Cathedral*

Every year in Chichester from around May to July, adult and young peregrine falcons can be seen swooping in and out of their nest in the spire. See p. 74 for details.

# GOODWOOD AERODROME CAFÉ ⑧ ROOFTOP

## *Free views across the historic airfield and raceway*

*The Goodwood Motor Circuit, Chichester, West Sussex, PO18 0PH*
*01243 755066*
*goodwood.com/aerodrome*
*Daily 9pm–5pm February to November, 9pm–4pm December and January*
*Admission free*

If we talk about the Goodwood Estate, it is likely that Goodwood House, horse racing and motorsport first spring to mind – particularly its three-day celebration of vintage motoring at the Goodwood Revival and its modern Festival of Speed. We don't tend to think of its historic aerodrome – or Goodwood airfield as it's also known. However, it is from this overlooked setting the roots of Goodwood Estate's motorsports grew.

Today, Goodwood Aerodrome operates a busy flying school out of a fancy new building, opposite the historic motor circuit. It includes a café, which not many people know has a rooftop viewing platform looking out over the historic airfield. Depending on the weather, visitors can watch the planes take off and land – from nostalgic Second World War Spitfires, Hurricanes and Harvards to modern Cessnas and even helicopters. If you do not have a head for heights, you can enjoy the view across the airfield from the café's lower ground terrace.

After watching the planes, feel free to wander around the aerodrome building areas as well as the motor circuit paddock. Here you will find a converted NAAFI wagon serving breakfasts, lunch and snacks (see p. 228). Picnics are also allowed on the banks of the track near the Motor Circuit Café.

Not far from the Aerodrome Café, in a corner of the motor circuit paddock, is the Goodwood Memorial Garden, a hidden ode to the forgotten Brooklands racetrack and various racing drivers associated with it. Most people do not know it is there (see p. 82).

## *An airfield created to help with the Second World War effort*

The Goodwood airfield was originally created on Goodwood Estate land donated by Goodwood heir, Freddie March, to help with the Second World War effort. Known at that time as RAF Westhampnett, it was active from July 1940 to May 1946 as a Battle of Britain station. It was also home to 43, 129, 145, 602 and 616 Squadrons who operated Hawker Hurricanes, P-51 Mustangs, and Supermarine Spitfires.

Flying training began at Goodwood in 1940 when young pilots were taught operational flying techniques in Hurricanes and Spitfires. The first operational sorties – attacks made by defending squadrons – were also launched from RAF Westhampnett, and carried out by the Fighter Groups of the US 8th Air Force in alliance with the allies.

After the war, March decided that the airfield's perimeter road would be converted into a racing circuit. It opened in September 1948 and hosted Britain's first post-war motor race.

# THE GOODWOOD MEMORIAL GARDEN ⑨

*A hidden ode to a lost age of racing*

*Goodwood Aerodrome*
*Goodwood Motor Circuit, Chichester, West Sussex, PO18 0PH*
*01243 755066*
*goodwood.com/aerodrome*
*To view from the outside only*

Tucked in between the motor circuit paddock car park and the new Aerodrome Café at Goodwood is a curious walled garden. On closer inspection, you will see it is filled with headstones.

The Goodwood Memorial Garden remembers drivers and pilots associated with the Goodwood Road Racing Club. It also commemorates the legendary Brooklands racing circuit in Surrey which opened in 1907. It was the first purpose-built racing circuit in the world, and its design was an incredible feat of engineering at the time. It is so significant it is a listed historic monument, open to view at the Brooklands Museum.

At 30.5 metres wide, 15 metres at its highest point, with a steepest incline of 26 degrees, racing here was the ultimate thrill – if you had the money that was. Brooklands attracted wealthy racing enthusiasts and a social scene which reflected the tastes of Britain's upper-middle classes and celebrities.

As well as Dame Barbara Cartland (see box below), Goodwood Estate heir and the man behind Goodwood's racing passion, Freddie March, was a member of this elite club. He was obsessed with motoring, a regular at the track and an accomplished driver, winning the 500 Mile race for Austin in 1930, and the Double Twelve for MG in 1931.

Brooklands and its scene thrived until 1939 when the Second World War broke out and damage forced it to close. After the war, Freddie March decided to turn the Goodwood Estate airfield's perimeter road into a racing track. It opened in September 1948 with Britain's first post-war motor race and is still well used today.

One of the largest headstones in the garden commemorates McLaren racing team founder, Bruce McLaren. He lost his life in 1970 while testing the team's Can-Am challenger, the M8D, at Goodwood. The memorial headstone was unveiled by his widow, Pat, 22 years after the tragedy on 2 June 1992, alongside scores of McLaren's former team members, rivals and friends. McLaren's death was a massive blow to his close-knit team, who continued working to create the superteam and automotive empire.

## *A speedy woman*

Socialite and writer Barbara Cartland was a Brooklands racing circuit regular and organised the first all-female race at the track. She also got permission for a ladies' reading room to be set up, for lady racing drivers to relax in during the racing, which you can see inside on a visit to the Brooklands Museum in Weybridge, Surrey. Visit brooklandsmuseum.com for details.

# BLAKE'S COTTAGE

⑩

*A seminal Romantic artist's former seaside retreat*

*Blakes Road*
*Felpham, Bognor Regis, West Sussex, PO22 7EE*
*To view from the outside only*

Having created some of the most iconic and influential works of British art and poetry, William Blake, the English painter, printmaker and poet, is now recognised as a seminal figure of the Romantic Age.

According to the Blake Society, he lived in nine houses in his lifetime, only two of which survive: one in London's West End at 17 South Molton Street, and this one in the village of Felpham in Bognor Regis, West Sussex.

In 1800, Blake moved from Lambeth in south London into this humble thatched cottage on the Sussex coast with his wife, Catherine, to escape the city and take up a job illustrating books. The move also marked the start of the most important period in Blake's life and career. It was in this cottage that he wrote some of his best-known poetic works, including *Milton: A Poem* and the words to the hymn *Jerusalem*.

He also depicted the cottage several times in his paintings; for instance, in a rare watercolour landscape showered in sunlight, now held by the Tate Britain. He is also known to have described the house in letters to a friend: "No other house can please me so well, nor shall I ever be persuaded, I believe, that it can ever be improved in beauty or use ... the sweet air and the voices of winds, trees, and birds, and the odours of the happy ground, make it a dwelling for immortals. Work will go on here with God-speed".

The cottage is largely unchanged from when Blake lived in it between 1800 and 1803, with the same beamed interiors and original doors, and even the vegetable patch which can be seen in some of Blake's sketches.

Although the cottage is currently closed to the public, its owner, the William Blake Trust, plans to open it as a visitor centre in the future. The Trust bought the property in 2015, following a two-year campaign backed by comedians Russell Brand and Stephen Fry and writers Alan Moore and Neil Gaiman, a patron of the society. It raised the £520,000 to buy the cottage from its owner, 90-year-old Heather Howell.

Blake spent his last years in Fountain Court off The Strand in London's West End. The apartment block no longer exists having been demolished when The Savoy Hotel was built in the 1880s. He died in London on 12 August 1827, leaving uncompleted the cycle of drawings inspired by Dante's *Divine Comedy*. He was buried in an unmarked grave at Bunhill Fields in Finsbury, London.

# CLIMPING BEACH

(11)

## *Wild, overlooked and unspoiled*

*Climping Street, Climping,*
*West Sussex, BN17 5RN*

So much of the Sussex coastline is heavily built up, that it is hard to imagine how it once was. Climping Beach, a magical stretch of beach in West Sussex, is one of the very few places along the coast which is relatively undeveloped.

With its mix of dunes, shingle and (when the tide is out) expanses of sand, Climping Beach makes for an alluring discovery. It feels a million miles away from the busier town beach resorts nearby and also feels like you have found your own secret beach: it is highly likely you will have it almost, if not all, to yourself when you pay a visit.

You will find this piece of south-coast paradise set mid-way between Bognor Regis and Littlehampton, hidden at the end of a quiet country lane. To get to it, turn off the A259 Bognor Road into Climping Street, signposted Climping Beach, and continue along to the end of this country lane, at the end of which is the car park.

What makes the Climping Beach landscape so special is that it is home to one of only two dune systems in West Sussex (the other is at Witterings). Both are heavily protected under the Site of Special Scientific Interest label, which also encompasses its vegetated shingle, sand flats, a small patch of saltmarsh and a nature reserve at West Beach, just east of Climping.

Wildlife-wise, sand lizards and four kinds of Nationally Scarce burrowing bees and wasps are just some of the rare species attracted to the dunes. The vegetated shingle, though common locally, is considered internationally rare, and is also used by a species of ant registered at risk of extinction on the Red Data Book or the Red List of Threatened Species; while the nearby sand flats host large numbers of migratory waders in winter. One of the strangest discoveries you might make, however, might be the black eggs of the thornback ray, known as mermaid's tails, which are easily mistaken for stag beetles.

### *Climping on screen*

One of Climping Beach's claims to fame is that it was used as a location in a couple of episodes of *Doctor Who* in the 1960s and 70s.

## NEARBY

### *East Beach Café*

For a delicious lunch in a unique architect-designed setting which challenges your notion of seaside café architecture, head towards Littlehampton. The East Beach Café resembles a giant piece of driftwood (or Hobbit house, depending on how you look at it) and serves creative seaside dishes to enjoy with a view over East Beach. See p. 226.

# FORD MATERIALS RECYCLING FACILITY TOURS ⑫

## *Lifting the lid on the recycling process*

*Education Centre*
*Ford Road, Ford, Arundel, West Sussex, BN18 0FL*
*recycleforwestsussex.org/education/*
*Open for West Sussex community groups and schools*
*To book, call 01903 712620 or email fordeducation@viridor.co.uk*
*Admission free*

Recycling is a hot topic right now, but still, so many of us are not entirely sure what we can and cannot put into our recycling bins – or what happens to it once it has been collected.

This might be why the average West Sussex household wastes 59kg of recycling by putting it into the wrong bin. That is 22,000 tonnes a year of recycling going to waste, potentially sent to landfill.

Everything that does make it into a West Sussex recycling bin is processed at the £15-million Ford Materials Recycling Facility near Arundel. Run by Viridor, it was developed as the flagship sorting facility under its 29-year household waste recycling contract with West Sussex County Council, which was signed in March 2004.

It is an incredible, almost non-stop, operation. It has sorting and separating technology capable of sifting through 100,000 tonnes of

material each year, splitting it into 13 different material streams ready for reprocessing or resale.

Sorting through all of our old cans, bottles, cardboard and paper is not all that happens here: the Viridor team also offers West Sussex-based groups, schools and individuals the chance to learn about the process and go behind the scenes during free educational visits. They are so popular that they tend to get booked up well in advance.

Visits start with an eye-opening presentation led by education and communication officer Jo Norman. It demystifies the entire recycling process from start to finish in an engaging way, peppered with thought-provoking facts and figures. Recycling at home is tackled in detail, with all those niggling questions answered. Like, what to do with toothpaste tubes and lightbulbs, and why it is essential that everything is clean, dry and loose before being put out for recycling, to name but a few. You certainly leave well-informed with plenty of useful takeaway tips – like the paper scrunch test: if the paper stays scrunched, it is likely it can be recycled.

Visits finish with a behind-the-scenes hard-hat tour of the extraordinarily loud materials recycling facility room, which ultimately provides the context for the information given in the presentation.

Health and safety levels are high at the facility, so headphones, a high-vis vest, hard hat, safety goggles and gloves must be worn. Kitted out, visitors are then led up some metal stairs and along a walkway up to a viewing platform, to take in the view across the gargantuan operation. The network of zig-zagging conveyor belts crammed with our recycling is a sobering sight.

# REMNANTS OF A JAMES BOND FILM SET ⑬

## *A fictional villain's lair*

*Amberley Museum*
*New Barn Road, Amberley, Arundel, West Sussex, BN18 9LT*
*01798 831370*
*amberleymuseum.co.uk*
*Wednesday to Sunday 10am–4.30pm*

Amberley Museum is a fascinating, popular and vast open-air industrial heritage attraction in West Sussex, with an unusual setting in a former chalk quarry complete with original kilns and mine shafts.

It is also home to a little-known site with Hollywood connections, namely the remnants of a 1980s James Bond film set, and some other ephemera relating to the film, which most people tend to overlook for other exhibits.

Old signage used in the film can still be seen hanging above one of the mine shafts which was used in scenes in the 1985 Bond film, *A View to a Kill*, starring Roger Moore, Grace Jones, Christopher Walken and Tanya Roberts.

It was used as the entrance to the fictional Main Strike Mine, owned by Bond villain, Zorin, played by Walken. This was supposedly his company's headquarters in California, where Zorin carried out his plan to blow up the competition in Silicon Valley and the Crystal Lakes. Scenes inside the mine were filmed at Pinewood Studios in London.

The mine entrance at Amberley features in various shots in the film: when Zorin's workers are transporting goods into the mine on green crates and are digging into the tunnels underground; when James Bond and Stacy Sutton (Roberts) sneak into the mine hidden in carts; when May Day (Jones) escapes out of the mine just before she is blown up; and in the background when Stacy is captured and pulled into Zorin's Zeppelin airship.

The museum was closed for three weeks during the summer of 1984: two weeks to build the set, one week for filming with a production crew of 200 people. You will find a collection of behind-the-scenes photos of the cast and crew relating to the film in the Railway Hall building. Although they are not on show, the museum also owns two Hudson Hunslet locomotives which the Bond film crew used to push and pull the mine carts.

## *Sussex elsewhere on film*

Various locations in Sussex have been used in TV programmes and films. Petworth House featured in the 2014 film *Mr Turner* starring Timothy Spall; Brighton City Airport terminal building (see p. 206) was used to portray Le Bourget airport in Ron Howard's 2016 *The Da Vinci Code*; Lancing College (see p. 198) was used as the backdrop for scenes in the 2008 film *Brideshead Revisited*; Eastbourne pier offered a backdrop to various scenes in *Harry Potter and the Goblet of Fire*; while the beach at Cuckmere Haven in the Seven Sisters Country Park (see p. 56 and p. 58) was used in the film *Atonement*.

# MILL LANE TREE TUNNEL

⑭

## *A fairy-tale walkway*

*Mill Lane, Halnaker, Chichester, West Sussex, PO18 0LX*

Sussex has no shortage of magical woodland to explore. There is one particular area near Chichester, however, with a naturally occurring feature that is fun to discover: an ancient path to a windmill with a hobbit-like tunnel of trees at the end.

The tunnel of trees runs along Mill Lane, which you will find on the Windmill Trail, a fully signposted public footpath near Halnaker (pronounced Ha'naker), a hamlet a few miles north of Chichester in West Sussex, in the South Downs National Park.

The lane follows an ancient track along the old London to Chichester Roman road – now called Stane Street. Over the years, it has sunk down, worn away by centuries of footfall. It is not long before you are surrounded by a magical tunnel of trees.

The route then leads walkers through the lanes of Boxgrove, onto Halnaker and footpaths skirting the Tinwood Estate, before crossing onto Mill Lane and bearing left 128 metres up to Halnaker Hill itself, for spectacular views across the countryside and on a clear day, to the sea. It also makes a nice spot for some star gazing on a clear night (see p. 20).

Up here is also where you will find the Halnaker Windmill, built in the 18th century and functioning as a mill until it was hit by lightning in 1905. It lay abandoned for years, but today is gradually being restored to its former glory. The original mill was built for the Duke of Richmond and the Goodwood Estate, and was first recorded in 1540. At the top you will find a bizarre looking structure – a Neolithic earthwork called a causewayed enclosure, which is also home to a World War Two observation point.

Wildflowers carpet the hill in spring, and some of them really rare, including the pyramidal orchid and common spotted orchid. Red admiral, marbled white and common blue butterflies also like to make an appearance at this time of year, as well the odd skylark or buzzard swooping overhead.

## *Branching out: tree tunnels around the world*

The world is full of tree tunnels. Some of the most impressive include one known as "dark hedges" in Northern Ireland, created from a row of 18th-century beech trees surrounding the path to the manor house of the Stuart family, said to be haunted by the Grey Lady; the 800-foot long tunnel of 19th-century oak trees leading up to a Greek Revival house at the historic Oak Alley Plantation on the Mississippi River in Louisiana; a tunnel of mangrove trees shading canals in the fishing community of Roatan in Honduras which can be seen on boat trips, and the otherworldly tunnel of yews at Aberglasney Gardens in Wales, made up of a row of ancient trees knotted together, planted in the 18th century.

# THE TRUNDLE

⑮

*For secret free views over the Goodwood horse-racing grandstand*

*The Trundle*
*St Roche's Hill, South Downs National Park, West Sussex*

St Roche's Hill in West Sussex near Chichester is 206 metres high and set amid ancient woodland. At the summit is an ancient Iron Age hillfort called the Trundle, which not only offers a window into ancient history, countryside views and walking opportunities: in the summer, it becomes a grassy grandstand from which to watch the horseracing at Goodwood – for free.

From this vantage point, you get a clear view over Goodwood Racecourse which hosts 19 unique race day events, including the flagship Qatar Goodwood Festival, affectionately known as "Glorious Goodwood".

Organised racing at the Goodwood Estate dates back to 1800. This was when the Goodwood Estate owner at the time, the 3rd Duke of Richmond, would organise racing events to entertain local army officers at the Harroway, a narrow ridge just to the east of the Trundle. The following year, he built the triangle course north of the Harroway for a private race meeting and built a thatched grandstand in 1802 for the first public meeting. Although it has been re-laid and improved over the years, the course at Goodwood remains largely unchanged from the one originally built.

While you eat your sandwiches and sip a chilled glass of rosé atop the Trundle waiting for the racing to start, ponder the ancient history of the landscape. The Trundle is an Iron Age fort amid a landscape shaped by glaciers at the end of the last Ice Age. As temperatures increased, a wildwood replaced sparse grassy tundra landscape, which over time saw people moving to it to exploit the rich hunting and gathering opportunities, making small clearings for seasonal hunting camps.

The first clue that people inhabited the Trundle dates to around 4,400–4,200BC. This is when our early nomadic ancestors began to farm the landscape and started the transition to a more settled existence.

## *Secrets of the High Woods*

A lost Roman Road and Neolithic caves are just two of the ancient landscape features to discover on the Trundle, as part of the Hidden Landscape walking trail. It is part of a project called "Secrets of the High Woods" organised by the South Downs National Park Authority, which used laser surveying to uncover lost archaeology and the heritage of people who lived and worked on the South Downs landscape throughout the ages. To find out more about the project and download a trail leaflet, visit the South Downs website at southdowns.gov.uk/enjoy/walking/hidden-landscape-trails.

# ST ROCHE'S ARBORETUM

16

## *An overlooked parkland walk*

*West Dean Gardens, West Dean, Chichester, West Sussex, PO18 0RX*
*01243 818215*
*westdean.org.uk*
*March to October: weekdays 10.30am–5pm, weekends and bank holidays 9am–5pm*
*November to February: weekdays 10.30am–4pm, weekends and bank holidays 9am–4pm*

Most people visit West Dean Gardens near Chichester to wander around its formal gardens and see inside its working Victorian glasshouses. Another way to enjoy this bucolic Sussex estate is to take a 4-km circular parkland walk around its incredible arboretum.

The path is almost 2 km from West Dean College which you reach by following a route across the estate's front lawn, eventually passing through an avenue of redwood trees.

The walk consists of three tracks – the pheasantry, forest and central tracks, each winding their way through and around undulating parkland and hidden glades, taking you past shrubs and specimen trees.

These include tulip and horse chestnut trees of which West Dean Gardens holds two National Collections. Other highlights include a centenarian oak tree along the forestry track close to the entrance, a 100-plus-year-old horse chestnut tree further along, as well as an impressive 25-year-old Davidia (handkerchief tree) on the central track.

It is as beautiful in autumn and winter as it is in late spring when the rhododendrons and azaleas bloom, and all throughout the summer. It also has jaw-dropping views across the Sussex Downs and over West Dean College of Arts and Conservation.

## *Secrets of St Roche's*

There are two unusual sights to discover while you are walking around the arboretum. The first is a simple slab in a shady spot amid Himalayan rhododendrons inscribed with the word 'poet'. This is where West Dean's little-known eccentric owner, Edward James, is buried. James inherited the West Dean Estate when he was just 25 years old – along with an entire village, 6,000 acres of woods and farmland and several other houses. He became disillusioned with upper-class elite life, trading it for one less conventional, eventually becoming an avid supporter of the avant-garde Surrealist movement. This included bankrolling the careers of Surrealist artists, Salvador Dalí and René Magritte.

The second sight to spot is a bizarre looking chalk boulder on a gentle slope, this is one of the 13 chalk stone sculptures by artist Andy Goldsworthy which form the Chalk Stones Trail (see p. 102.)

# SURREALIST TREES

⑰

*A bizarre artistic legacy of West Dean's eccentric founder*

*Spring Garden*
*West Dean Gardens, West Dean, Chichester, West Sussex, PO18 0RX*
*01243 818215*
*westdean.org.uk*
*March to October: weekdays 10.30am–5pm, weekends and bank holidays 9am–5pm*
*November to February: weekdays 10.30am–4pm, weekends and bank holidays 9am–4pm*

With its manicured English country garden-like landscape, Surrealism is not the first artistic genre you would associate with West Dean Gardens at first glance. A little dig into its history books, though, and we quickly learn that its eccentric founder, Edward James, had strong ties with the Surrealist art movement as one of its patrons. He also considered Surrealist artists Salvador Dalí and Rene Magritte as acquaintances.

As well as his grave in St Roche's Arboretum (see p. 96), James' Surrealist legacy also lives on in a hidden corner of West Dean Gardens in the form of two fibreglass sculptures, known as the "Surrealist trees". Hidden near the bridge in the west of the Spring Garden, one on either side of the river. Despite their irregularity, they do not actually stand out.

According to the head gardener at the time, Ivan Hicks, James wanted to perpetuate trees which were due to be felled because of disease and old age by encapsulating the standing timber in fibreglass. A sculptor called Ralph Burton was commissioned to carry out the work in 1972 and 1974. The timber has since rotted, leaving the fibreglass shells, forming the sculptures around the original trunks.

Elsewhere in the Spring Garden, there are plenty of secret walkways, flint bridges and hidden benches to discover. It was redeveloped over a period of years with West Dean gardeners adding a pond.

The rustic summerhouse at the westerly end was restored to its early 19th-century glory with moss walls, seaweed decorations, heather ceiling and thatched roof. It makes a perfect spot for a quiet rest. Parts of this area date back to the Regency period, including a series of flint bridges. The laburnum and ivy tunnel makes a shady walkway in the summer sunshine.

## *Get surreal in Sussex*

Other evidence of the Surrealist movement in Sussex can be found at Farleys House, nicknamed "House of the Surrealists" after its owners' Surrealist work and connections (see p. 44). Farleys also runs courses in Surrealist photography and cooking, and even hosts an annual Surrealist Picnic (see p. 46), for your chance to dress up and cook surreal food.

# BEEDING TOLL HOUSE

(18)

## *A curious miniature cottage*

*Weald and Downland Living Museum*
*Town Lane, Chichester, West Sussex, PO18 0EU*
*01243 811363*
*wealddown.co.uk*
*Daily October to March (except 24 and 25 December) 10.30am–4pm, April to September 10.30am–6pm*

The fascinating Weald and Downland Living Museum in West Sussex is home to an intriguing little building that resembles a miniature cottage. This is a perfectly preserved example of a building known as a toll house. Toll houses were built in England, Wales and Scotland during the 18th and early 19th centuries and formed part of the system of road maintenance managed by groups known as Turnpike Trusts. These groups set up by Parliament had the power to stop the public highway with gates, bars, and turnpikes to collect tolls which would pay for the roads and their maintenance.

Originally, this example was located in the village of Upper Beeding and was moved to the museum in 1968. This was to protect it from further damage after an incident with a lorry. The missing front section and chimney have been reconstructed from photographic evidence.

The Beeding Toll House as it has become known, is characteristic of toll cottages in the triangle between Worthing, Horsham and Shoreham and is the last surviving one of this type – all the others have been demolished for road improvements.

It was built to control what the official turnpike records call "the new road to avoid Beeding Hill, from Beeding through Old Shoreham to the south-east corner of the Sheep Fold in the parish of Kingston-by-Sea", a diversion authorised by Parliament in 1807. It is thought that the cottage was probably built at the same time.

The new road eased the route through the South Downs by avoiding the severe gradient of Beeding Hill, considerably improving the movement of traffic between the older centres of population of the western Weald, such as Petworth and Steyning, and the booming Brighton of the Prince Regent's era. The road remained turnpiked until 1885, and together with the Horsham–Steyning–Beeding road, has the added interest of being the last public road in Sussex on which a toll was levied.

Tollhouses varied architecturally but were typically one storey high with two or three rooms. In 1840, according to Parliamentary papers, there were over 5,000 toll houses operating in England. These were sold off in the 1880s when the turnpikes were closed. Many were demolished but several hundred have survived with the distinctive features of the old tollhouses still visible.

> As well as toll houses, the General Turnpike Act of 1766 also made it compulsory for turnpike trustees to instal milestone markers (see p. 42). Unfortunately, many were lost or destroyed during the Second World War after they had been removed for security reasons. Those which have survived are in constant danger of being lost in road-widening schemes.

# CHALK STONES TRAIL

(19)

## *A novel way to discover the South Downs*

*From Cocking Hill to West Dean, West Sussex*
*To download a trail map:*
*walkandcycle.co.uk/sussex/Trails/50-99/SUSSTR0088.pdf*
*2.5 hours to walk*

There are plenty of ways to discover the landscape of the South Downs. None is more novel than the self-guided walking route of the Chalk Stones Trail that takes you up and over its undulating hills and through dense forest in search of a bizarre set of giant chalk stone sculptures.

The Chalk Stones Trail is a collaboration between Scottish environmental artist Andy Goldsworthy and the Pallant House Gallery in Chichester (see p. 76). It is designed to celebrate the local landscape known for its chalk, a rich natural material found in abundance in Sussex, usually hidden from sight.

There are 13 stone sculptures in total to discover on the trail. Each one is set at various points along the 8-km trail that starts from the bus stop at Cocking Hill and ends at West Dean College – or vice versa – and takes about 2.5 hours to walk, if you manage not to get lost.

The stones were installed in 2002 and look very different now from the early days when they were bright white and clean. Today, almost 20 years later, they have grown into their surroundings, and some of them have been almost completely reclaimed by nature, which adds to their elegance.

One of the chalk stones can be found hidden amid the trees in the overlooked parkland walk around St Roche's Arboretum at West Dean Gardens (see p. 96 for more information).

## *Goldsworthy: an artist well known for creating artworks exclusively from natural materials*

Goldsworthy is well known for creating artworks exclusively from natural materials. Many of his creations are ephemeral, some lasting no longer than a few hours, or even minutes, preserved only as photographs.

The Chalk Stones Trail is, for example, similar to a project he created called Midsummer Snowballs – of which there is a book – commissioned to celebrate the Millennium. It consisted of 13 one-tonne snowballs made entirely out of snow which Goldsworthy collected over the winter months in Scotland and kept in cold storage.

The snowballs were then released onto the pavements of London's financial district for people to discover on their way to work. They were filled with a variety of natural elements, from feathers, seeds, and pinecones to rusted metal, which were revealed as the snowballs melted.

# THE POTAGER

20

## *Art of the vegetable*

*Woolbeding Gardens*
*Brambling Lane, Woolbeding, Midhurst, West Sussex, GU29 9RR*
*0344 249 1895*
*nationaltrust.org.uk/woolbeding-gardens*
*March to November: Wednesday to Friday 10.30am–4.30pm*

With its slightly secret location – in that you cannot make your own way directly there, you must meet a guide in a local car park and get on a minibus – Woolbeding Gardens in Midhurst is a real hidden Sussex gem in itself.

It is also home to an attention-grabbing horticultural feature known as the potager, made entirely out of lettuces.

You will find it inside the formal garden rooms not far from the William Pye fountain. When you spot a particularly impressive vegetable patch that pretty much stops you in your tracks, you know you have found it.

Traditionally, potager is the French term for an ornamental vegetable or kitchen garden, created to make the growing of food attractive and aesthetically pleasing. It is thought to have originated in Medieval France, among the monasteries. "Potage" literally meaning a thick and substantial soup, all the ingredients for which were grown in the kitchen garden or potager.

The central area of the potager at Woolbeding consists of around 1,200 lettuces surrounded by chives – the design is changed three times a year, with each design lasting around 10 weeks until the lettuces begin to 'hearten' and bolt in warm weather.

The designs are created using two or three contrasting varieties of lettuce, such as Nymans, a dark purple lettuce, Lolla Rossa, a frilly loose leaved green variety turning to purple, Tom Thumb, a dark green butterhead, and finally Lettony, which has frilly pale green leaves.

At the centre of the design is a shrub called *buxus sempervirens* which is clipped into the shape of a swan.

If you visit the gardens throughout the season, you get to see the potager change month by month. In the summer, you will experience fragrant sweet peas in bloom in a multitude of colours, artichokes that reach incredible heights, runner beans on eight-foot bean poles and asparagus, which once picked by mid-June provides a soft feathery effect. Underplanting varies from season to season.

Frequently used plants include squashes, courgettes, cucumbers, herbs, nasturtiums and marigolds. In the surrounding beds, there is a wide abundance of fruit, vegetables and flowers, including Ballerina apples creating a gateway, and gooseberries fanning the back wall to soften the brick work.

Woolbeding Estate and Gardens was given to the National Trust in 1957 and leased to Simon Sainsbury in 1972. With his partner Stewart Grimshaw, he restored the 17th-century house and worked with contemporary garden designers to create the elegant country retreat and gardens we see today.

As well as the potager, there is a jaw-dropping surprise around every corner on a walk around this magical 23-acre horticultural wonderland.

Highlights include the Tulip Folly which looks like it was plucked straight from a Parisian park, and the Long Walk which features a series of views dotted with quirky artistic architectural structures, like a ruined abbey, a hermit hut and a statue of a river god.

# THE TOWER ROOM

(21)

## *A romantic Renaissance art studio*

*Cowdray Heritage Trust*
*River Ground Stables, Midhurst, West Sussex, GU29 9AL*
*01730 812423*
*cowdray.co.uk/historic-cowdray/the-tower-room*
*Open for various courses throughout the year*
*See website for details or email towerroom@cowdray.co.uk*

In the heart of the South Downs National Park, Midhurst has a feature that distinguishes it from any other Sussex town: the charred skeleton of a Tudor mansion house called Cowdray Park, which was once home to the Montague family. Built in 1542, it was destroyed in 1793 by a fire.

Until recently, visitors were free to wander around the remains, or join a guided tour. Today, you can still walk around it for a sense of its scale, but due to structural safety issues, it has been fenced off, which means you cannot get up close.

Another way to enjoy this mystical setting is to sign up to an art class at the Renaissance Art Studio, with a unique setting at the top of a tower. Most people do not realise that this place exists.

It is set in the old kitchen tower, the only part of Cowdray Park to avoid fire damage and was refurbished by Viscountess Cowdray in the last decade. The studio is run by artist-in-residence David Cranswick, who leads classes which explore techniques and artistic styles developed by the great master painters of the 16th and 17th centuries, when Cowdray was in use.

Workshops include Dutch still life painting which explores the traditional materials and techniques used by the Dutch masters of the 17th century. The Alchemy of Colour workshop offers the chance to make your own paints and looks at how pure pigments are extracted from their natural sources in the form of earth, rocks, roots and berries, and how these are then purified and transformed.

After Cowdray Park was razed to the ground, it remained in its ruinous state, largely untouched until 1909 when the 1st Viscount Cowdray commissioned a restoration project. This move is credited with saving the ruins from total collapse.

The property was opened as Cowdray Park Ruins to the public in 2007 after an intricate two-year restoration, stabilisation, access and interpretation project. Other parts of the building which you can see clearly as you walk around are the buck hall, chapel and gatehouse.

# PETWORTH COTTAGE MUSEUM (22)

*An ode to life as a Petworth Park Estate seamstress*

*346 High Street, Petworth, West Sussex, GU28 0AU*
*01798 342100*
*petworthcottagemuseum.co.uk*
*April to October: Tuesday to Saturday 2.30pm–4.30pm*

The picturesque village of Petworth in West Sussex and its community was established around the 700-acre Petworth House Estate in Petworth Park.

One of the 500 cottages in the village owned by the estate – each identifiable by the mid-brown painted woodwork – has been turned into a museum which celebrates life as an estate worker.

The Petworth Cottage Museum – or "Mrs Cummings' Cottage" as it is also known – opened about 25 years ago when a local resident decided it would be a good idea to contrast life in Petworth Park with the life of an estate worker. Along with a couple of friends, she persuaded Lord Egremont to lease a cottage.

Research led them to find out that, at the turn of the 1800s, the lady who lived here had been a lady called Mary Cummings, a seamstress who worked at Petworth House between 1901 to 1930, hence its nickname "Mrs Cummings' Cottage".

The building dates back to the 1600s but was taken over in the 1800s by the estate, with Mary moving in in the late 1800s.

It is not a museum in the traditional sense: rather a house that has been restored and furnished to how it might have been in about 1910 when Mrs Mary Cummings lived in it. Nothing you see in the cottage is newer than 1910, and it all comes from Petworth and other estate cottages.

It has been set up to feel as though Mrs Cummings has just stepped out: the fire is lit, the table laid for tea and the kettle is on the stove.

Each room is packed with things to look at: the scullery complete with a stone sink, wash copper, laundry equipment and period kitchen furniture and utensils, while the cellar has an original coal hatch to the street.

Upstairs, "Mary" is at her sewing machine in the work room. It is also where we find her bedroom and are given a glimpse inside her wardrobe at what she might have worn to church on a Sunday. A highlight might be the little window in the children's attic room with a rooftop view of Petworth across to Petworth House.

Mrs Cummings is buried in the St Anthony and St George churchyard, in the village of Duncton, south of Petworth.

## *Safety in numbers*

Street numbering in Petworth might seem haphazard in that it does not use the traditional system of odd and even numbers on separate sides of the street. Instead, door numbers indicate the order in which the estate took over the premises for the estate workers.

# WILD SUSSEX

23

## *A unique conservation project*

*The Wood Yard*
*Stopham Road, Pulborough, West Sussex, RH20 1EB*
*wildsussex.co.uk*
*Saturdays 9am–5pm*

Wild Sussex might look like just a roadside pop-up shop in a barn, but it is far more than that. It is a collaborative community project that supports the local rural economy by promoting and protecting sustainable, traditional skills at risk of disappearing forever, particularly coppicing, which is essential for creating biodiversity.

Up until the First World War, nearly all woodlands in Britain were managed in this way, but there are now only a small number of skilled craftspeople continuing this traditional practice, so many of our woodlands are now not as diverse as they could be.

Coppicing involves sections of a woodland being felled on a rotational basis over seven years. This allows sunlight to flood the woodland floor, causing dormant seeds and other light-loving pioneering plants to germinate, creating new habitats which attract different wildlife. As each section matures, the plants, insects, birds, reptiles and mammals that prefer a more open environment are able to move around the woodland as needed. The regrowth of the trees results in a continual source of wood for various products.

"Traditionally though, for coppicing to be financially viable, the timber produced in this way would be sold to craftspeople to use to make various products ranging from charcoal, baskets, thatching spars, hurdle fencing, and other crafts", says Sam Claydon, one of the founders of Wild Sussex.

He explains that "coppicing and making craft take up a lot of time and many of the few makers left don't have enough money – or time – to set up their own shops, run websites and do the marketing required to sell their products on a large scale".

Wild Sussex supports local coppice workers and traditional craftspeople by selling their products and running workshops on topics such as coppicing and making plant supports out of willow and hazel branches reaped from the coppicing woodlands.

"I really wanted to remind people of the traditional skills found right here in Sussex and that beautiful, long-lasting products can be made locally and sustainably. We are also almost completely plastic-free. When you buy one of our products you are supporting the continuation of traditional crafts, maintaining livelihoods, and conserving the local Sussex landscape", adds Sam.

# BEDHAM CHURCH SCHOOL RUINS

24

*The ghostly shell of an abandoned architectural gem*

*Wakestone Lane, Pulborough, West Sussex, RH20 1JR*

Nestled amid enchanting woodland not far from the village of Petworth is what looks like an abandoned church-like building.

If you approach it heading east along the A272 and turn right towards Bedham on Wakehurst Lane, the first sight of it through the trees makes for an eerie yet alluring discovery.

Used as a school as well as a church (at the same time), this abandoned architectural gem is also a reminder of the long-forgotten but once thriving hamlet of Bedham, home to a farm and a number of little cottages.

If you venture inside its crumbling walls, leaves crunching underfoot, you will see a plaque which reads: "For the worship of Almighty God, in gratitude for many blessings. This building was erected by William Townley Mitford of Pitshill in 1880".

At its peak, the curious building was used regularly by the community. During the week, it was the village schoolhouse. On Sunday, the school-related paraphernalia was tidied away and the chairs turned to face east ready for the Sunday service.

As a school, it is thought that around 60 pupils from the local area were taught here by three teachers. It is also thought that adults and children took lessons at the same time, in classes separated by a curtain.

In 1925, its use as a school ceased, as children moved to larger schools being built in the area. It was used as a chapel for a few decades longer until it closed in 1959.

## *A forgotten community for artists*

Country cottages in England could be bought for as little as £100 in the early 1900s, so Bedham became popular with artists of limited means who wanted to escape the city. One of these artists was the leading composer of his time, Edward Elgar, who was enticed down from London by his friend, the author Ford Madox Ford. Elgar lived in a cottage called Brinkwells for four years. It is here where he is said to have composed his last four great works: the *Violin Sonata in E minor*, the *String Quartet in E minor*, the *Quintet in A minor for piano and string quartet*, and the *Cello Concerto in E minor*. The works are said to have been inspired by a strange local legend relating to the nearby woods. This is where a curious clump of trees is said to be the remains of Spanish monks who engaged in sacrilegious ceremonies and were struck by lightning.

# THE WEY AND ARUN CANAL

㉕

## *A restored section of London's lost route to the sea*

*Wey and Arun Canal Centre*
*High Street, Loxwood, Billingshurst, West Sussex, RH14 0RD*
*01403 752403*
*weyarun.org.uk*
*Public boat trips on Saturdays, Sundays and bank holiday Mondays from early April to late October*
*weyarun.org.uk/content/boat-trips for more information on special themed cruises and private trips*

When we think of canals, we imagine lazy, sunny days walking or cycling on the towpath, a picnic on a leafy bank, or a holiday chugging on a narrowboat. In Victorian times, however, the picture could not have been more different: canals were functional beasts, used primarily to transport cargo between London and the provinces.

In the 19th century, it was possible to travel from London to Littlehampton on the south coast by boat along commercial canals. The Wey and Arun Canal was a vital link on this route connecting London and the busy river Thames to the English Channel and beyond. It opened in 1816 but eventually fell out of use and became abandoned. However, in its heyday in 1839, it carried 23,000 tons of cargo between the city and countryside. It was vital in that it was the only link between the south coast and the River Thames in a once-extensive system of inland waterways covering England and Wales.

When the railway first came to Sussex, it had little impact on the canal, but in 1865 the line between Guildford and Horsham opened in direct competition with it, which meant that it could not compete for speed and convenience. By 1868, canal traffic had virtually ceased and in 1871 an Act of Abandonment was passed. Slowly, section after section, the canal became abandoned. By 1970, it was no more than a stagnant, muddy, overgrown depression in the ground.

Today, it is gradually being restored by the Wey and Arun Canal Trust with the completed sections open to the public. So far, 10 of the 26 locks have been renovated, with plans to restore them all in the future. Half of the surrounding towpath has also been rejuvenated and is now an atmospheric green corridor for wildlife. It is also a long-distance walking and cycling route called the Wey-South Path, a guide to which you can download from the website opposite.

Visitors are encouraged to bring their own canoes, kayaks, paddleboards and small craft to use on the water. The Trust also runs various boat trips on its three curiously named boats: *Josias Jessop*, *Zachariah Keppel*, and *Wiggonhot*. Its timetable includes regular scheduled trips, private rides as well as novelty themed trips, such as "cream tea voyages", "picnic and Pimms supper cruises" and "the ploughmans and Pimms celebration".

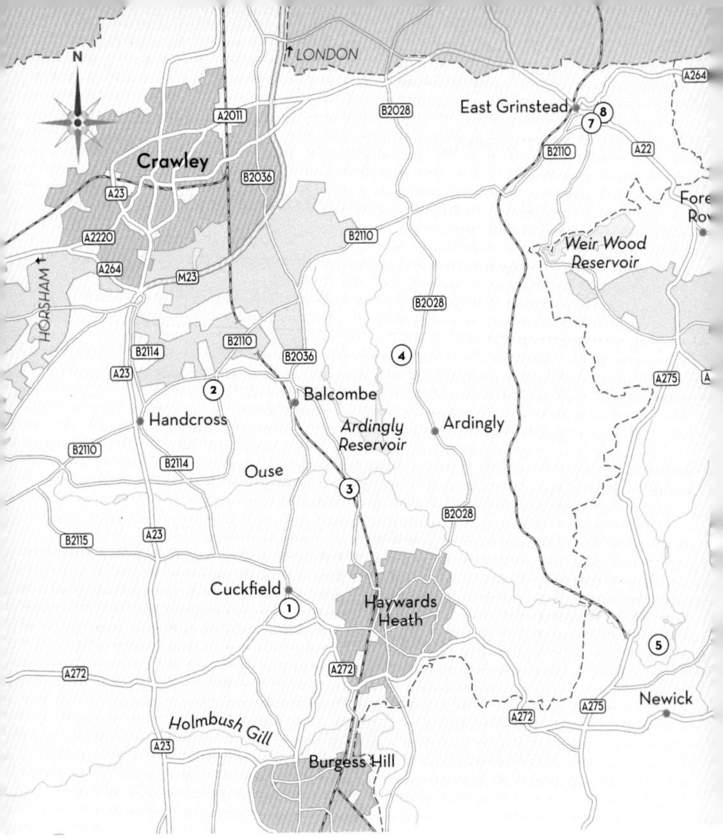


# *Crawley to Crowborough*

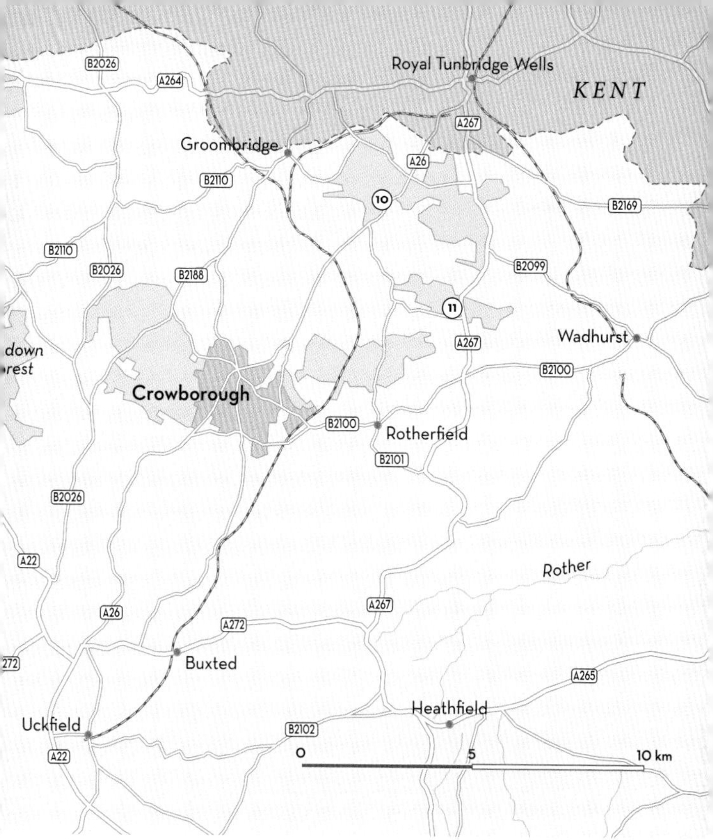
Royal Tunbridge Wells
KENT
Groombridge
Wadhurst
Crowborough
Rotherfield
Rother
Buxted
Heathfield
Uckfield
0
5
10 km

# CUCKFIELD BUNKER

1

## *A secret underground time capsule*

*Newbury Lane*
*Cuckfield, Haywards Heath, East Sussex, RH17 5AA*
*01273 973220*
*facebook.com/Cuckfieldnuclearbunker/*
*Open on select days between April and September*
*See the Facebook page for details*

Hidden in the corner of a field near the Holy Trinity churchyard in Cuckfield is a strange looking cordoned off structure with a hatch. It might not look like much, but this is the entrance to a once top-secret underground nuclear bunker which has been restored as a museum and is open to inquisitive visitors at various times during the year.

The bunker was originally built in 1962 as a Royal Observer Corps post, one of more than 1,500 built in the 1960s and 70s, where the immediate effects of a nuclear blast could be monitored along with radioactive fallout. This is the site from which a four-minute warning would have been sounded to alert the population of an incoming nuclear attack during the Cold War.

Although the bunker closed six years after it opened to save money, it was reopened two years later after flooding caused another bunker in nearby Ditchling to close.

Cuckfield Bunker was used until 1991 when the Royal Observer Corps was stood down. It remained locked up and abandoned until 2007, when Mark Russell and Ed Combes set about restoring it and filling it with memorabilia.

Visitors descend the 4.5-metre entrance shaft by ladder. At the bottom, they emerge into an underground space consisting of a small antechamber, a storage area and main bunker room – about the size of a single-car garage in total – filled with equipment, paperwork and rations that would once have been used.

It is sobering to discover all the nuclear war-related ephemera on show. There are nuclear weapons training manuals, a bomb power indicator used to record the pressure of a blast wave following a nuclear explosion. There is even a radiation meter for measuring the amount of radiation outside using a sensor inserted through a hole in the ceiling.

"It's taken us over 10 years to fill the post with the equipment that would have been used," says Combes.

"There wasn't much in here when we first went inside although what we've saved is now on display, like the wooden cupboards and desks and some paperwork. We sourced a lot of the ephemera from eBay, at auction and antique shops. Other collectors and museums have made donations, but we're always looking out for other gems to add to our collection."

# WINGS MUSEUM

2

## *An aviation museum with a macabre twist*

*Unit 1, Bucklands Farm, Brantridge Lane, Balcombe, East Sussex, RH17 6JT*
*07769 688064*
*wingsmuseum.co.uk*
*Tuesday to Sunday 10am–5pm*
*Occasionally open at night*

Inside a cavernous old barn, hidden between Balcombe and Handcross in the East Sussex countryside, is an aviation museum – with a twist.

Most museums on the themes of aviation and motoring tend to revolve around showing off collections of perfectly restored memorabilia and machinery. The Wings Museum, however, is unusual in that part of the collection features Second World War plane crash wreckage, some of it recreated into scenes resembling the crash sites they were originally salvaged from.

Although the idea of looking at recreated plane crash sites on a day off might sound bizarre, a visit here in fact makes for an absorbing experience – even for those with no interest in the war or aviation history.

The sound of wartime-era music playing in the background adds to the feeling of nostalgia and even makes browsing a pleasant experience.

The museum was started by the Hunt brothers who became interested in Second World War relics as young boys on a family holiday to Norfolk, when their dad discovered a Browning machine gun on the edge of an old airfield at Felixstowe. This is, of course, on display in the museum along with their many other finds from the old airfields of East Anglia. So enthusiastic are they to preserve and rescue items relating to our war-time aviation history, they have travelled all over Europe for their hobby: to France, Belgium, Germany, Norway and even Siberia.

Their collection is utterly vast, including not just the dioramas, but cabinets bursting with memorabilia each with a unique story which enthusiastic volunteers cannot wait to tell you. All of it is centred around a complete restoration of the fuselage from a Douglas C-47 Skytrain used in the HBO series, *Band of Brothers*, into which visitors are free to walk.

The most hard-hitting exhibit is in the V-Weapon Room which, alongside recovered components of the flying bombs, chronicles the Dora slave labour camp that built the infamous V2 Rockets that rained down across England.

There is also an unusual "gift shop" where you can buy your own piece of plane wreckage, engine parts, and even bullets complete with certificates of authentication detailing the crash site and those who lost their lives on board – if you are into that sort of thing.

Outside, do not overlook the little shed filled with old refurbished two-way radios. The museum is also occasionally open at night.

# OUSE VALLEY VIADUCT

③

## *A Victorian masterpiece*

*Borde Hill Lane*
*Haywards Heath, East Sussex, RH17 6QP*

Travelling by train through the Ouse Valley over the Ouse Valley viaduct is a magical stage of the journey between London and Brighton. It feels like the train slows down – even though it does not – as the trackside trees give way to sweeping views across the valley lowlands carved out by the river Ouse. It is a breath-taking experience that sees most commuters looking up from their books and iPhones to drink it in.

Arguably though, it is the viaduct itself underneath which is the star of the show, which you cannot see if you are on the train.

Not only is it an incredible feat of engineering, it is also a magnificent architectural piece of art. The Victorians were well known for their wildly ambitious infrastructure projects, of which this is a great example. Built 180 years ago, and spanning 450 metres, it consists of 37 symmetrical hollow piers, or arches. When you look through them all at once – you have to climb up into one of the arches to do so – the bridge looks as though it goes on and on forever. Although it is easy to assume this design feature was the result of deliberate engineering ingenuity, it was actually the result of a cost-saving exercise.

Even so, 11 million bricks were still used to construct this gargantuan infrastructure project. What is equally remarkable is that all of them were brought over from Holland by barge and transported along the river Ouse. Looking up at it from the ground, over 30 metres in the air, is an arresting sight – one that is particularly mesmerising when one of the four or five trains an hour thunder overhead.

The Ouse Valley Viaduct was designed by lead engineer, John Rastrick, together with the architect of the Brighton to London railway, David Mocatta, who added a stone cornice with balustrade along the top of the viaduct and erected eight classical pavilions, four at each end.

It has not always looked so impressive though. In 1996, it underwent a £6.5 million renovation project which took three years to complete. This saw a number of improvements which required precise detailing. For example, harder-wearing limestone was imported from Bordeaux to ensure the closest match with the existing Caen stone in the balustrades and pavilions. Some of the piers had to be reconstructed using handmade bricks made in a number of different sizes to match the Victorian brickwork, then set in a sand, cement and lime mortar; stainless steel anchoring was also used to firmly attach the new stone to the old.

# MILLENNIUM SEED BANK

④

*A giant subterranean bunker of genetic diversity*

*Royal Botanic Gardens*
*Wakehurst Place, Selsfield Road, Ardingly, West Sussex, RH17 6TN*
*01444 894100*
*nationaltrust.org.uk/wakehurst*
*Daily 10am–3.30pm*

There are over two billion seeds from more than 38,000 species at the Millennium Seed Bank at Wakehurst in West Sussex. All of them are stored at sub-zero temperatures inside an underground vault large enough for 38 double decker buses, and robust enough to survive the worst natural or man-made disasters imaginable.

It is an incredible project and scientific operation – home to one of the greatest concentrations of living seed plant diversity on earth. Yet most people overlook this mind-blowing hub of scientific activity in favour of a wander around the gardens of Wakehurst Place.

It seems appropriate that the utopian-sounding Millennium Seed Bank is housed within several shiny domed buildings that resemble futuristic greenhouses. The laboratories and offices are in two separate wings, flanking a light and airy open space, known as the visitors' hall. From here, through windows, you can watch the Millennium Seed Bank scientists at work. You also get a good view down to the entrance of the underground vaults where the seeds are stored (pictured).

Seed collections arrive at the seed bank in varying states, sometimes attached to fruits, sometimes clean. The collections usually also include a voucher specimen – parts of plants or whole plants – that can be used to identify the origin of the seeds. The collections are immediately moved to a dry room for processing where they are cleaned, X-rayed, counted, and banked in sealed glass containers.

The scientists' work also includes testing which varieties will grow and under which conditions, and the optimum conditions for seed germination after storage. they also experiment with cryogenic freezing techniques which involve using liquid nitrogen to flash freeze the seeds and prevent any decay.

The seeds are also given out to researchers from all over the world who use them to study whether better crops can be grown; for example, by cross-breeding with wild varieties. Staff also provide help and advice to botanists from developing countries to assist them in setting up their own national repositories.

Initially set up at Kew Gardens in 1980 as the Kew Seed Bank Facility, the project moved to Wakehurst in 2000. Its main goal is to collect seeds from 75,000 plant species representing 25% of known flora. It is in the second phase of its plan, having already achieved the original partnership goal to bank 10% of known flora a year early in 2009. It also aims to collect seeds from all the UK's native flora, which it also does locally (see p. 12), as well as to carry out further research into conservation and preservation of seeds and plants, and act as a focal point for research.

# SKYGLADE

⑤

## *A peaceful hidden spot for cloud gazing*

*Parkland area*
*Sheffield Park and Gardens, Uckfield, East Sussex, TN22 3QX*
*01825 790231*
*nationaltrust.org.uk/sheffield-park-and-garden*
*Open dawn to dusk*

Most people head straight for the showstopping Capability Brown landscaped garden at Sheffield Park, with its incredible lake surrounded by glorious trees. It is a sight to behold especially in autumn when the leaves turn a rich mix of orange and red. There is another equally beautiful aspect to Sheffield Park, however, that remains less explored. This is the surrounding 250-acre parkland area scattered with curious sights, including one which children and adults alike will enjoy discovering.

Hidden in a copse through a gate is the Skyglade, a peaceful place for pausing and taking in the beauty of the vast open sky. It consists of eight 2.5-metre-high wooden panels arranged in a circle, each one set at a compass point. They are made of Sussex oak, felled from the same tree, with the bark left on to blend in with the veteran oak trees surrounding them.

Simply choose a panel, lean back, look up and take in the expanse of sky above you, the shape of the clouds, and the relaxing sounds of nature. The Skyglade is occasionally open at night, too, when it becomes the setting for star-gazing events led by local astronomers throughout the year.

Once you have distinguished your cirrocumulus from your cirrostratus and your nimbostratus from your cirrus, and if you can peel yourself away from this tranquil experience, there are other curious sights to discover in the parkland area.

These include an art trail created by local artists and schoolchildren, supported by the National Lottery Heritage Fund, and a well-preserved pillbox from the Second World War set into the hillside at the bottom of Spring Field. There is also the Ringwood Toll natural play trail which follows a circular loop in an enclosed woodland copse. This is where children can build a den, climb trees, play on a seesaw, slack line or stepping stones, and sit on a storytelling chair, to name but a few activities.

Alternatively, a three-mile estate walk offers the chance to soak up the tranquillity and curiosities of the parkland area as a whole, offering sweeping views of the Sussex countryside, that takes around 1.5 hours to complete. See here for details: nationaltrust.org.uk/sheffield-park-and-garden/trails/estate-walk-at-sheffield-park

On your way out, do not miss the incredible 300-year-old sweet chestnut tree in the car park.

# OWL'S HOUSE

⑥

*A miniature tree house*

*Five Hundred Acre Wood*
*Ashdown Forest, East Sussex*
*ashdownforest.org*

A.A. Milne, author of the world-famous *Winnie-the-Pooh* stories about a honey-loving bear, lived near the village of Hartfield, not far from Five Hundred Acre wood in Ashdown Forest. This area became the inspiration for the fictional Hundred Acre Wood, where Christopher Robin and his childhood friends – Winnie the Pooh, Rabbit, Tigger, Piglet, Eyeore and Owl – lived out their adventures together.

Most people who visit Five Hundred Acre Wood to follow in Pooh's footsteps head for the famous wooden bridge over the river Medway. This is where Pooh and his friends played Poohsticks; a game in which sticks are dropped in a river and raced under a bridge. But there is another little-known clue to this forest world, which children will particularly love to discover.

About halfway into Five Hundred Acre Wood, a little way up an old beech tree is a miniature front door with the words "Owl's House" on the front. This marks the entrance to the fictional home of Owl, the eldest of Christopher Robin's friends. Owl is known to enjoy talking a lot and is considered a know-it-all, presenting himself as a mentor to his friends, even though the advice he offers is usually questionable.

In the *Winnie-the-Pooh* stories, Owl's house is called The Chestnuts, and described as an "old-world residence with great charm", with amenities like a pull-bell and a fancy doorknocker on the front. Unfortunately, in *The House That Pooh Built*, Owl's House is blown down, so Eyeore finds him a new one, which turns out to belong to Piglet – the door to which you can spot in the forest not far from Owl's, at the bottom of a tree.

Another curiosity of Ashdown Forest can be found in Gills Lap at the top of the High Weald. It is a plaque commemorating Winnie-the-Pooh creator, A.A. Milne and the stories' illustrator, E.H. Shepard.

If you want to venture a little further on between Gills Lap and the little village of Hartfield on the northern edge of the forest, you will be able to see A.A. Milne's former home, Cotchford Farm, which he bought in 1925 as a place to bring up his six-year-old son Christopher, known to the family as "Billy Moon", on whom he based the character of Christopher Robin. Although you cannot visit the house, it is thought that there is a sundial in the garden decorated with characters from the Pooh stories. The property was later controversially owned by former Rolling Stone bassist Brian Jones.

# QUEEN VICTORIA HOSPITAL COLLECTION ⑦

## *The hidden story of a little-known pioneering surgeon*

*East Grinstead Museum*
*Old Market Yard, Canteloupe Road, East Grinstead, West Sussex, RH19 3BJ*
*01342 302233*
*eastgrinsteadmuseum.org.uk*
*Wednesday to Saturday 10am-4pm; Sunday 1pm-4pm*
*Admission free*

The East Grinstead Museum in East Sussex couldn't be more unassuming, tucked out of sight behind the high street. But if you stumble on it, you'll discover that it's home to an incredible archive of memorabilia called the Queen Victoria Hospital collection.

Some of it has been used to create a fascinating permanent exhibition, *Rebuilding Bodies and Minds*, celebrating the hospital and the incredible work of a little-known pioneering surgeon who worked there, Sir Archibald McIndoe.

During the Second World War, the Queen Victoria Hospital in East Grinstead became one of four specialist emergency medical service units in the country used to treat burned air crew. A maxillo-facial unit was established at the hospital by McIndo, the civilian consultant in plastic surgery to the Royal Air Force at the time. It's where he became famous for pioneering a remarkable treatment regime for severely burned airmen, famously known as his "guinea pigs".

In July 1941, McIndoe formed the Guinea Pig Club as a social support group for his "guinea pigs"', the burned airmen he treated at the hospital during the Second World War. It still meets annually in a local pub called The Guinea Pig, close to the museum.

The exhibition tells the story of how McIndoe helped rebuild the faces and the lives of these brave airmen after their terrible ordeals. It features lots of memorabilia like old photographs, documents, entries in journals (even McIndoe's surgical implements and operating table are on show), taken from the vast collection donated to the museum. Before it found its new home at East Grinstead Museum, it had been sitting in storage at a local furniture depository after the unit closed.

Not to be overlooked is a cabinet of incredible illustrations depicting surgical procedures. These were created by a young surgical artist called Mollie Lentaigne. She worked at the Queen Victoria Hospital in the Second World War alongside McIndoe and his team and drew hundreds of medical illustrations depicting the plastic surgery McIndoe carried out.

Everything from both of these collections is registered in the museum's database alongside a photograph of each item. Visitors are free to search through the archive in the museum's research room. Other items in the collection that aren't on show can be seen by arranging an appointment with the museum's curator.

Alternatively, on the first Friday of every month, the museum offers 30-minute tours of the hospital collection exhibition, bringing to life Sir Archibald McIndo's incredible story and his work at the Queen Victoria Hospital. The tour highlights important objects and significant events in the development of burns treatment and plastic surgery.

# JOHN MASON NEALE'S GRAVE

⑧

*Resting place for a world-famous Christmas carol composer*

*St Swithun's Church*
*Church Lane, East Grinstead, East Sussex, RH19 3B*
*Daily 9am–5pm*

An easily missed secret of East Grinstead can be found in a quiet corner of St Swithun's churchyard next to the rose garden, where a grand tomb is surrounded by a manicured hedgerow, with the name John Mason Neale inscribed on the top.

It is a name we will most likely not recognise, although we will no doubt be familiar with his contribution to modern festive entertainment.

The warden of the nearby almshouse, Sackville College, between 1846 and 1866, Reverend John Mason Neale is said to have rescued the college from decline and decay and to have cared deeply about the residents: for instance, he set up an infirmary room upstairs next to the chapel so they could hear the services.

As well working as a local clergyman and serving the community, he wrote many well-known hymns and poems. He also wrote Christmas carols, including the words to one of the most famous – *Good King Wenceslas.*

Since it was created in the 1800s, it has become one of the best loved Christmas carols ever written, having even been covered by The Beatles, REM, Joan Baez, Bing Crosby and Tom Jones. It has also been parodied by both Spike Milligan and the *Horrible Histories* team.

Neale wrote the carol for the Feast of Saint Stephen, better known to us as Boxing Day. Traditionally this was a day of charitable giving on the day after Christmas Day, not a time for bargain hunting in department stores.

The carol tells the story of Wenceslas, a 10th-century Catholic Duke of Bohemia, also known as Vaclav the Good, who sets out on a fanciful journey through a snowy forest to bestow alms to a poor peasant on the Feast of Saint Stephen.

Although Neale wrote the lyrics to the carol in 1853, the melody is said to be much older, dating back to the 13th century and first published in the 1582 Finnish song collection *Piae Cantiones* – it was originally a lot faster, written as a lively spring dance called *Tempus adest floridum* ("the time is near for flowering").

Slowed down, it turns out it makes the perfect accompaniment for carol singers trudging through the snowy darkness.

Another reminder of Neale can be found inside St Swithun's Church: on the left-hand wall as you face the altar, a stained-glass window depicts Neale in the middle panel, wearing the green robe he wore when working in Sackville College Chapel.

King Wenceslas was martyred after being assassinated by his wicked brother Boleslaw the Bad. His remains are interred in St Vitus's Cathedral in Prague. He is also immortalised in a statue located in one of Prague's main city squares: Wenceslas Square. Installed in 1912, the statue was designed by Czech sculptor Josef Vaclav Myslbek.

# HAMMERWOOD PARK

⑨

## *Led Zeppelin's former mansion, where things are not quite as they seem*

*Hammerwood*
*East Grinstead, East Sussex, RH19 3QE*
*hammerwoodpark.co.uk*
*Open for 1.5-hour-long tours at 2pm on Wednesdays, Saturdays and bank holidays, 1 June to 30 September (includes tea and cake in the Elgin Room)*

The rolling Sussex countryside is scattered with manor houses, but none as intriguing as Hammerwood Park near East Grinstead.

At first glance, it might look like any other house of its stature, built as an ostentatious display of wealth in which to entertain the upper classes. Hammerwood, however, represents so much more, which owner, David Pinnegar, reveals on colourful and unconventional house tours, in which he encourages visitors to understand the logic behind the house's unusual architecture.

For one, it is a complete illusion, built to appear bigger than it is from a distance – it is actually only one-third of the size it looks from afar. The columns on the wings are half the size of those in the middle, to make them appear as though they are set back a huge distance, while the columns on the temples are tapered to make them look taller.

For another, tours start outside at the back, which is actually the front, where Pinnegar – who is passionate about the property's Greek origins – is keen to point out the stonework which emulates the Temple of Athena at Paestum in southern Italy and friezes replicating the Borghese Vase, depicting Dionysus carrying a drunk man, which Pinnegar links to Hammerwood's agricultural heritage as a hunting lodge.

Hammerwood is one of only two British buildings built by Benjamin Henry Latrobe, the Yorkshire-born architect and polymath who designed the US Capitol building and the porticos at the White House. Built in 1792, it was described as one of the first examples of the Greek Revival movement in Britain, complete with Doric columns and classical inscriptions.

It has had several owners throughout the years, including British rock band, Led Zeppelin, who in the 1970s planned to turn it into a music complex featuring studios and apartments for band members and their families, but instead left it to become derelict, from which it was rescued by the Pinnegars.

Inside, the main hallway is covered with a trompe-l'œil mural painted by two young French artists for Hammerwood's bicentenary in 1991, the same year Pinnegar's eldest son George was born (depicted as a cherub halfway up the stairs).

The tour also leads into a few rooms, each one home to a musical instrument which Pinnegar is not shy to play. This is his way of highlighting the series of summer concerts they run every year, alongside tours, to help preserve the heritage and for future generations who "are at risk of smartphone deterioration", says Pinnegar.

# ERIDGE ROCKS

⑩

*Once the setting for elaborate Victorian gatherings*

*Eridge Rocks Nature Reserve*
*1 Warren Farm Lane, Eridge, Tunbridge Wells, East Sussex, TN3 9JG*
*sussexwildlifetrust.org.uk/visit/eridge-rocks*

The Eridge Rocks are a series of large boulders set in 24 hectares of dense ancient woodland in the East Sussex High Weald. In 1086, the time of the Domesday Book, the High Weald had the highest density of woodland in the country.

At 10 metres high in some cases, it is hard to imagine that these great sandstone cliffs were once so overgrown you could not see them. But when Sussex Wildlife Trust bought the area in the late 1990s, they were almost hidden.

The neglected rocks had been reclaimed by nature, completely covered by rhododendron, bamboo and acacias. All of it was originally planted by the Victorians, who had long held a fascination for the rocks. According to various historic accounts, they were often used as the setting for frivolous stage plays and elaborate dinner parties, featuring liveried footmen who stood to attendance at the bottom.

Today, the rocks and surrounding woodland have been restored and are known as the Eridge Rocks Nature Reserve. However, unless you are into rock climbing or live locally, the fact they exist may even come as a surprise to many Sussex residents.

This ancient landscape is heavily protected as a Site of Special Scientific Interest, and is a habitat for an array of small life forms which thrive in most damp conditions: tiny plants, mosses, lichens and fungi. Many are so rare that they are only found at a few sites in Europe.

Visitors explore the reserve on trails that wind their way through and around the rocks. Come spring, the landscape bursts into bloom with primroses, green-winged orchids, sweet vernal grass, yellow archangel, wild garlic, common dog violet and cuckoo pink. A rare variety of orchid known as the coralroot can also be spotted growing in bluebell drifts.

In the winter, water escaping from the porous rocks freezes and forms impressive icicles. In summer, butterflies such as the silver-washed fritillary and white admiral are spotted in coppiced areas. Male longhorn moths can also be seen flying around in groups in the sunshine, and adders basking in the bracken.

Other highlights of a visit to the Eridge area include the Saxonbury Tower, a fairy-tale like folly on the Eridge Park Estate, home to the Marquess of Abergavenny and his family, which looks like it has been plucked out of a Disney film set (see p. 138). Also worth seeing is the Eridge Folly, a mysterious underground cave-like structure cut into a sandstone cliff, with two entrances, on the north side of a fishing lake off Sham Farm Road, Eridge.

# SAXONBURY TOWER

11

*A fairy-tale folly in a medieval deer park*

*Eridge Park*
*Rotherfield, Crowborough, East Sussex, TN3 9HT*

Britain is awash with follies, those whimsical architectural features built to add interest to many an English country estate garden. They were hugely popular in the 18th-century and designed in complete contrast to the strict social hierarchies of country house life. Outside in the garden, there was a different world where the rules could be relaxed.

Follies, as a result, are often unusual and unconventional in design. They might resemble Roman temples, ruined Gothic abbeys, Egyptian pyramids (see p. 160), or fairy tale-like towers, like this one close to Tunbridge Wells in East Sussex, which looks like it has been plucked out of a Disney film set or from a Bavarian castle and then added to the Sussex woodland landscape.

The Saxonbury Tower was built in 1928 on the Eridge Park Estate, home to the Marquess of Abergavenny and his family. Built as an observation tower, it marks the southernmost and highest point of the estate and is distinctive for its tapered design, conical roof and arrow slits – all features which give it its fairy-tale quality.

Walking towards it through the atmospheric fern-filled woodland of oak, beech and birch trees, you half expect a handsome prince to gallop past on horseback at any moment, on his way to rescue Rapunzel who emerges to let down her hair.

Although you cannot go inside the tower, it is nice to imagine pushing open the castle-like wooden door and climbing the sandstone spiral staircase five floors to the top to take in the views.

The Eridge Park Estate is itself steeped in history, reputedly being the oldest enclosed Deer Park in England. It is listed in the Domesday Book under the name of Reredfelle and the ownership of Odo, the brother of William the Conqueror. It is also thought that visitors to the park included Henry VIII as well as by Queen Elizabeth, who stayed at Eridge Park for six days in 1573.

The village of Eridge is home to several other curiosities. These include the Eridge Rocks, 10-metre-high boulders once completely covered by foliage and abandoned but now restored and open as a nature reserve (see p. 136 for more information), and the Eridge Folly, a mysterious underground cave near a fishing lake off Sham Farm Road, thought to have once been a sand mine.

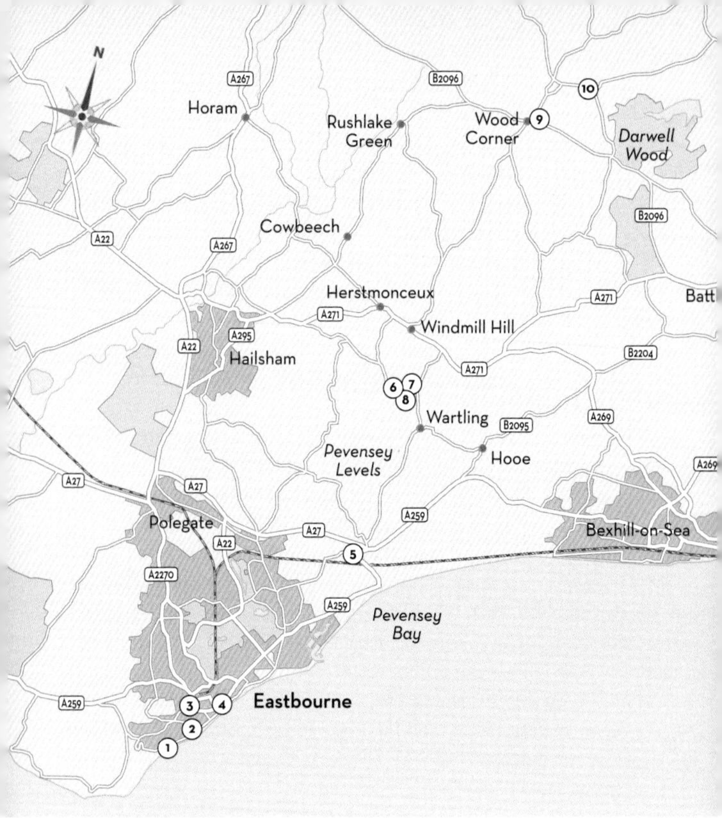


# *Eastbourne to Rye*

---

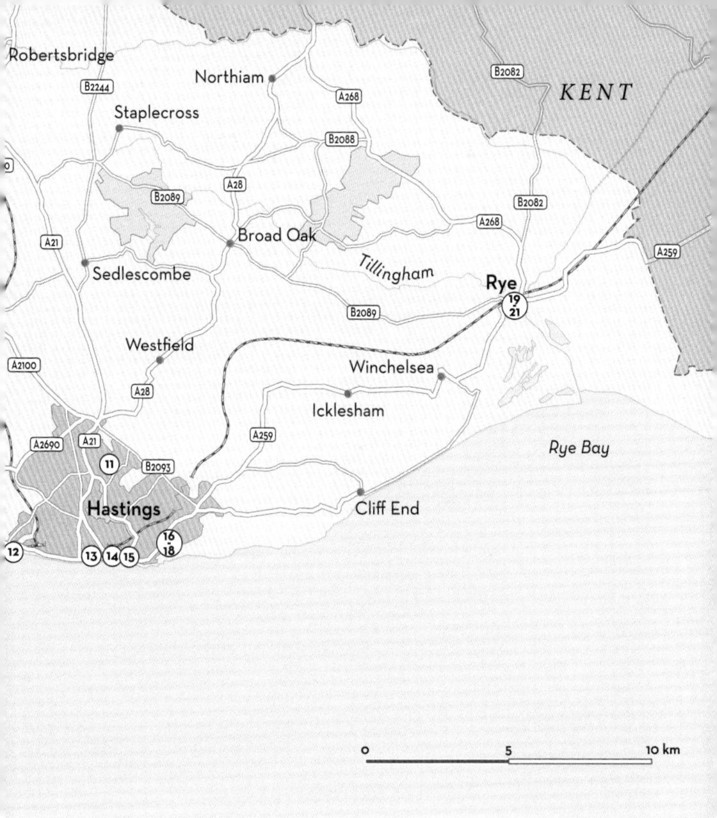
Robertsbridge
B2244
Northiam
A268
B2082
KENT
Staplecross
B2088
A28
B2089
B2082
A268
A21
Broad Oak
Sedlescombe
Tillingham
Rye
A259
19
21
B2089
Westfield
A2100
Winchelsea
A28
Icklesham
A259
A2690
A21
Rye Bay
11
B2093
Hastings
Cliff End
16
18
12
13
14
15
0
5
10 km

# THE ITALIAN GARDEN

①

*A secluded seaside sanctuary in a former quarry*

*53 King Edward's Parade*
*Eastbourne, East Sussex, BN20 7XB*
*Free*

Tucked behind Helen Gardens and the dramatic white chalky cliffs of Beachy Head, the Italian garden is an intriguing green sanctuary that makes for a charming surprise discovery on a trip to Eastbourne.

You will find it at the western end of the promenade by Holywell Retreat Beach. To reach it, head up one of the little tree-lined paths either off the South Downs Way or behind the Tea Chalet café. After a while, you will emerge into this beautifully secluded garden, complete with a wooded amphitheatre carved out of the cliff-face, Italian-style wooden pergolas and palm trees. It feels like you have walked into another realm, although the background sound of crisp fresh waves hitting the shoreline is a reminder you are still by the coast in Eastbourne.

The narrow path carries on, looping up and over the gardens taking you over a wooden bridge, with a view down to the main pergola and out over the entire garden. The garden was created in 1904 when quarrying was stopped after it was discovered that excavations were polluting a nearby pure water spring, which was essential for the town's water supply at that time.

The garden was redesigned in the Italianate style we see today in 1922. The work was carried out by First World War veterans, and included creating the pergolas and a larger sheltered platform with its view of the sea. This is said to have once housed the terminal equipment that controlled the transmissions of the Holywell-Dieppe underwater telegraph cable.

In the summer, the gardens come alive when the Eastbourne Operatic and Dramatic Society (www.eastbourneshows.co.uk) stage open-air performances of Shakespeare plays.

## *A chalet occupied by King George V and Queen Mary in March 1935*

Returning down the path from the garden to the Holywell Retreat Beach promenade just beneath the Tea Chalet, you will find some delightful old-fashioned whitewashed beach chalets, one of which was occupied by King George V and Queen Mary on separate occasions in March 1935, according to a plaque above the door of chalet number two. There are 69 of these brick-built chalets along the terrace, each with a kitchenette, and a water and gas supply. They are rented out annually and every so often one becomes free. There is a waiting list which you can join for £25. Phone the Eastbourne seafront office for more information, on 01323 410611.

# COASTAL CULTURE TRAIL

②

*Gallery hopping along the Sussex coast*

*coastalculturetrail.com*

The Coastal Culture Trail is a 29-km route that links three award-winning Sussex art galleries: the Towner in Eastbourne, the De La Warr Pavilion in Bexhill and the Hastings Contemporary.

You have the choice to explore the trail via three means: by bike, on foot or by train. All three routes offer magical sea views and take you through some of the most stunning coastal landscapes in the UK.

Cycling follows a route that takes you mostly along the coast, all the way from the Hastings Contemporary to the Towner and is pretty much traffic free between Hastings and Bexhill. The walking trail is also traffic free, with the exception of a small residential road in one of the villages. A regular train service links Eastbourne, Bexhill and Hastings – it takes about 30 minutes and you can take your bikes on the train.

You could do all three galleries in a day, or spend longer. Local B&Bs and bike shops coordinate bike and luggage delivery.

Gallery-wise, there are two levels at the Towner to enjoy, with excellent exhibitions of painting, photography, sculpture and found objects – including a permanent collection of local artist Eric Ravilious.

There is a contemporary café overlooking the grassy Devonshire Park Lawn Tennis club (where one of the main pre-Wimbledon women's tennis tournaments takes place every June).

If you start in Eastbourne, standing on the sunny promenade, you can actually see as far as Hastings – your destination 29 km away. It is easy to walk or cycle along the seafront, with the coastal track lasting for a good few kilometres.

The shingly beaches along the trail are vast, empty and windswept, the sea turquoise and still, and the landscapes similar to those in parts of Australia, until you hit Normans Bay 7 km from Bexhill: its pastel-coloured beach huts, popular campsite and the smell of piping hot chips wafting from a café are a reminder you are still in Blighty.

The trail takes you through Cooden Beach, a little seaside village filled with upmarket houses facing the beach and a couple of campsites, buzzing with activity. It is not far after this point that you reach Bexhill's De La Warr Pavilion art gallery. The café serves excellent and hearty portions of food, along with wine and ales on tap, and has a terrace overlooking the pretty bandstands along the seafront.

Some of the best cycling on the trail continues past Bexhill, through St Leonards and on to Hastings. This is in most part due to the wide and generous cycle lanes along the promenade that see you all the way into town. On the way, you pass the site of the Amsterdam shipwreck (see p. 164) and Hastings' new pier, before discovering the swanky Hastings Contemporary in an area known as The Stade.

# LITTLE CHELSEA

③

*A quirky nod to the elegant London neighbourhood*

*Grove Street and South Street*
*Eastbourne, East Sussex*

If you find yourself caught near Eastbourne's main shopping centre and prefer browsing independent shops to big chains, there is an antidote to this overt consumerism just around the corner.

Little Chelsea as it has become known, is an alternative dining and shopping scene hidden just two minutes from the main train station at Eastbourne. You will know you have found it as the architecture changes from modern shops and office blocks to traditional terraces, and the atmosphere starts to feel different.

The area is centred around two attractive shopping roads – Grove Street and South Street – known for their charming Victorian-era architecture and fun mix of independent shops, cafés and restaurants, not a chain in sight. It feels like the Old Town in Hastings or Brighton's colourful North Laine.

The best way to approach the area is on a lazy stroll, so you have time to take in the old shopfronts and wander in and out of the string of curious shops. These offer absolutely everything – from books to ballgowns, to musical boxes and giant cake creations.

A generous chunk of time should be saved to browse the half a million books or so that line the shelves inside and out, fill the floors, and crowd the stairwell at Camilla's Books. This incredible shop has been on the corner at 57 Grove Street since the mid-1990s. If you happen to visit on a Tuesday or Friday, you might catch a glimpse of the shop's resident parrot, Archie, who lives on the first floor and apparently loves a sing-song.

Meanwhile, time wasters are welcome at John Cowderoy Antiques on South Street which specialises in musical box restoration. There is also a fine collection of musical boxes on sale too, from Victorian Polyphon to Swiss – all antique musical box tastes are covered.

Not to be missed on South Street is the Incredible Cake Company whose windows are decorated with its amazing giant sugary creations you will not be able to walk past without stopping to stare at before heading inside for a taste and a coffee. If you prefer your coffee alongside some music, head to the Vinyl Frontier record shop just up the road which also has a café. They also have a bar with DJ nights, live music on Saturdays, quiz nights, and open mic poetry evenings.

There is a handful of independent art galleries to browse, too, before ducking up one of the residential side streets for a glimpse of the rows of colourful houses nearby.

# ROYAL HIPPODROME THEATRE BACKSTAGE TOURS

④

*Behind the scenes at Eastbourne's oldest theatre*

*108-112 Seaside Road, Eastbourne, East Sussex, BN21 3PF*
*01323 802020*
*royalhippodrome.com/event/theatre-tour*
*Open for tours on the first Wednesday of each month*

It is a sweltering summer night in 1883. There are 1,200 people in the audience, all smoking, eating, drinking. Ladies sit doused in perfume to mask the rancid smell. The gas lighting hums and flickers: there is no ventilation. Soon, those way up in the gallery are blinded by a smoky fug.

This was the reality of a trip to see a show at Eastbourne Hippodrome Theatre in the late 1880s, a poignant scene which our guide sets out as we look out into the audience from the stage on a backstage tour of this fascinating theatre.

This is just before we are encouraged to take note of a trapdoor on the stage floor, which it turns out was added to accommodate a show by Harry Houdini in 1905.

Curious participants on this quirky tour are whisked from the auditorium, behind the scenes into the props stores and dressing rooms, under the stage, into the dressing rooms, and up three flights of stairs to the flying floor – where the scenery curtains are operated – for an extensive understanding of how the Royal Hippodrome came to be and still operates today.

Underneath the stage, we can see where Houdini would have emerged having dropped through his trapdoor, alongside other performers at the time. This array would have included a lot of animals such as lions and elephants.

Today, this subterranean area is far less exciting, having become more of a storeroom for all kinds of theatre paraphernalia and also a makeshift costume department.

On one side, our guide points out that what is now a tiny cupboard used to store paint, was once the dressing room of the late entertainer, Bruce Forsyth, who is said to have hated this particular theatre, according to various reports from staff throughout the years.

Up several flights of stairs, we reach what is known as the flying floor. This is where we learn how the scenery is changed during performances: historically, it was carried out by out-of-work sailors, hence all the ropes and signage you see, which make it look much like a ship's deck.

The theatre was designed by Mr Charles Phipps, a famous London architect best known for his theatres. From the outside, it now looks more like a cinema or a bingo hall than a theatre, a move made to appease financial backers who preferred it to fit in with the surrounding architecture.

Inside, as we discover, it is a completely different story, with the interior partly modelled on Phipps' now famous Savoy Theatre in London, which opened in 1882.

# PEVENSEY GAOL COURTHOUSE MUSEUM ⑤

*The minutiae of the village*

*High Street, Westham, Pevensey, East Sussex, BN24 5LG*
*01323 733419*
*pevenseycourthouse.co.uk*
*March to October: Wednesday to Friday 11am–4pm,*
*weekends 1.30pm–4.30pm*

Set in Pevensey's curious former courthouse and gaol building on its chocolate-box High Street, the quirky Pevensey gaol courthouse museum is filled with a bizarre yet vast collection of memorabilia that celebrates the building's heritage and local life.

It is all crammed into the diminutive first-floor courthouse room, amazing in itself for two reasons.

Firstly, it is possibly the smallest courtroom you have ever seen. Secondly, it is kitted out with all the original courthouse furniture, including the dock and magistrate's benches, which remain in exactly the same position they were in when it was last used as a courthouse in 1886.

The dock is a particular hit with children who love standing inside it playing prisoner or pretending to pay a fine to be let out. Adults no doubt prefer lauding it over the courthouse from up on the magistrate's bench, lined with old parish and court records detailing crimes committed and punishments dished out, which make a fascinating read.

Elsewhere, other items of intrigue include the only surviving uniform worn by the Pevensey Beadle – one of the first types of policemen – 200 years ago, and a picture of a tough local lady called Betty Breach, the last prisoner of Pevensey gaol and an early feminist. She was arrested, and then released, after retrieving her alcoholic husband from the local pub and throwing the rest of his pint over the landlord as punishment for encouraging him to drink.

Even more ephemera fills cabinets in the judge's robing room off the main courthouse, mostly relating to Pevensey's local history. The collection is huge. There are old pens and quills, weights, a doll owned by a local girl in 1875, a gin jar from the same period, old clay pipes found locally, shot flasks, a starting pistol and tinder box, to name but a few.

Underneath the courthouse on ground level is the cold, stony but well-preserved gaol, consisting of two tiny cells, and an exercise yard complete with a window said to date back to Tudor times.

### *A haunted museum?*

Rumour has it that Pevensey Gaol Courthouse Museum is haunted. If suddenly you are overcome by the overpowering stench of whisky while perusing the memorabilia in the courthouse, chances are there is someone else in the room – a former jailor who is said to have enjoyed a wee dram or several to help him through the cold nights.

# PETER THE SHEEP'S GRAVE ⑥

## *A hidden memorial to a loyal woolly friend*

*Royal Sussex Regiment Memorial Garden*
*Herstmonceux Castle Gardens and Grounds, East Sussex, BN27 1RN*
*01323 833816*
*herstmonceux-castle.com*
*Daily from 15 February to 1 November: 10am–6pm April to September, 10am–5pm February, March, October, November*

Visitors wandering around the gardens at Herstmonceux Castle will discover a peaceful memorial garden to the Royal Sussex Regiment, not on the official map. It is located just north-west of the formal gardens, by following the avenue of chestnut trees towards higher ground.

This is a hidden gem in itself, home to a bizarre grave site which is not easy to spot – the well-worn simple stone slab set into the flower bed, with the name "Peter" etched on to it. This marks the resting place of a sheep.

Peter was apparently a Southdown lamb born in April 1914 at Applesham Farm, in Lancing, Sussex. Unfortunately, Peter's mother died while he was still a lamb, so Peter had to be bottle fed at the farm.

Four months later, the First World War broke out. Lieutenant Colonel Sir Claude Lowther formed a committee to recruit a Southdown brigade of four battalions numbering 4,000 men. In early September 1914, the first recruits joined, including one man with connections to the farmer at Applesham Farm, who gave Peter the Sheep to the 1st Southdown Battalion as a mascot.

Peter was taken on a series of recruiting tours with the battalion's band. He became quite famous and the men of The Southdown Brigade soon became known as "Lowther's Lambs".

During the war, Lowther's Lambs experienced exceptionally heavy casualties. On 30 June 1916, 365 men were killed or went missing, and over 1,000 were wounded in a diversionary attack just before the Battle of the Somme. By the spring of 1918, the Lambs were virtually wiped out.

Peter lived on after the war as a mascot on the Herstmonceux Castle estate until he died in around 1927, when he was buried here in the gardens of the castle. His grave was forgotten for decades until a gardener, called Fiona Wingfield, discovered it obscured by leaves and earth in 2004.

> The story of Peter the Sheep is explored in more details during a tour of Herstmonceux Castle, which is open to the public at various times during the year.
> Visit herstmonceux-castle.com-events-experiences/ for more information.

LATEST PICTURES OF THE SOUTHDOWNS.

1st AND 2nd BATTALIONS.

THE "LAMBS" AND THE OTHER LAMB. ONE OF THE MASCOTS. THIS IS THE PET OF E COMPANY.

THE SOUTHDOWNS AT DRILL: THIS IS THE FIRST PHOTOGRAPH PUBLISHED OF THE MEN IN UNIFORM, AND WITH RIFLES.

# RELICS OF THE ROYAL OBSERVATORY GREENWICH

7

## *The former home of time management*

*The Observatory Science Centre*
*Herstmonceux, Hailsham, East Sussex, BN27 1RN*
*01323 832731*
*the-observatory.org*
*Daily 10am–5pm October to March, 10am–6pm April to September*

It is little known that the Royal Observatory Greenwich was at one time located in the village of Herstmonceux in East Sussex, in a unique domed complex built especially for it. It's now home to the Observatory Science Centre, an interactive museum with over 100 hands-on exhibits which explore the themes of astronomy, forces, light, colour and time.

Visitors can still spot reminders of the building's former life as the Royal Observatory inscribed on some of the door handles and drainpipes: the year '1955' and a small, black-painted anchor. This is the logo of the Admiralty responsible for running the Royal Observatory Greenwich, which gradually moved from London to Herstmonceux between 1948 and 1958.

Visitors also have the chance to see the centre's telescopes, each one originally used when the building was the Royal Observatory Greenwich headquarters.

There are six in total, and although none of them carry out any serious research these days, three of them are used during the centre's regular stargazing evenings, allowing visitors to view the night sky through them. There is a Thomson 30-inch reflecting telescope in Dome A, a 13-inch astrographic refractor in Dome D, and a Thompson 26-inch refracting telescope in Dome E. The latter was built in 1896 and took 60,000 pictures of the night sky when it was in use from 1897 to 1988. It is also available to view during the day.

The Royal Observatory was founded in Greenwich in 1675 when the area was a village in open countryside outside London. As the population of the city grew and smoke from factories and houses continually filled the air, it needed to relocate to find clearer skies.

Its move to East Sussex took place over 10 years. This included designing the unique domed complex we see today, which consists of several domes clad in patinated copper, a feature intended to make the building blend into the Sussex countryside.

At its peak, over 200 people worked at the Royal Observatory Greenwich at Herstmonceux, and they lived in the local community. The six telescopes were operated by employees called "night observers". They were on duty every night, carrying out precision work which required great concentration and skill. The observatory was eventually downsized and moved to Cambridge in 1990, and then shut down completely in 1998.

# HANDLING BIRDS OF PREY

⑧

## *An unusual activity in a magical setting*

*East Sussex Falconry*
*Herstmonceux Castle, Halley Road, Herstmonceux, East Sussex, BN27 1RN*
*01323 485529*
*eastsussexfalconry.co.uk*
*Daily throughout the year*

The 15th-century Herstmonceux Castle with its Elizabethan grounds and 300 acres of surrounding parkland is the unlikely location for a Canadian University, as well as the former Royal Greenwich Observatory (see p. 154). It is also the setting for a bizarre but exhilarating activity that reflects its late-medieval heritage: falconry.

Falconry sessions at Herstmonceux are organised by East Sussex Falconry, a family business set up and run by head falconer Gerard Sulter and his wife, Gemma.

Gerard's interest in birds of prey began at the age of ten, when he became intrigued by golden eagles. "Around this time, I was so into birds of prey that I actually told my next-door neighbours that I was building an aviary for my pet golden eagle", says Gerard.

Although Gerard concocted the story, it was the start of his life-long interest, which he went on to research enthusiastically, finding out as much as he could about birds of prey and how to become a falconer.

East Sussex Falconry hosts various half or full-day experiences, each offering the chance to handle, feed, fly and learn about birds of prey – from Harris hawks and kestrels to peregrine falcons and even vultures.

Perhaps the most magical experience might be the chance to spend an hour holding and flying barn owls. "This is our most popular experience", says Gerard. Alternatively, purists and the less sentimental might be more interested in taking part in the company's overlooked but more authentic experience: the hawk-falcon hunting day, which celebrates the tradition of falconry as a sport, using birds of prey to hunt small animals like voles and mice, which is not demonstrated during any other of East Sussex Falconry's experiences, except this one.

## *Behind the scenes at Herstmonceux Castle*

As home to an international university, Herstmonceux Castle is not freely open to the public except on the odd day for public tours. Its gardens and grounds are open for visitors to explore all year, though. For more information, visit herstmonceux-castle.com/events-experiences.

# THE SUGARLOAF

9

## *Built on a bet*

*Near Wood's Corner*
*Dallington, Heathfield, East Sussex, TN21 9LD*

Next time you are driving along the road between Battle and Heathfield (B2096) near Wood's Corner in East Sussex, keep your eye out for a strange architectural sight – the top of a bizarre 10-metre-high conical construction sticking up from behind a hedge surrounding a meadow on Christmas Farm.

This is what is known as the Sugarloaf, a building that it is believed was built as part of a bet at some point in the 1800s. What is also intriguing about it is that, despite measuring only 4.5 metres wide, it was once inhabited, which is impossible to imagine when you are standing inside it – which visitors are free to do.

According to a plaque, which has since been removed, the building was inhabited from the mid-1800s until the 1960s. Local accounts recall that by this point it was in such bad condition it was almost demolished, until a "save the sugarloaf" fund was set up to pay for renovations. After it was repaired, East Sussex County Council took over the ownership and future upkeep of the building.

At one point it had two floors connected by a ladder – the location of the windows outside is a clue. There was also a lean-to kitchen. Information about previous residents is hard to come by, although local records show that the Crouch family lived in it during the late 1870s, while the Lulham family are believed to have been some of the building's last residents.

Known locally as "the sugarloaf" after the way sugar was delivered at the time in cones, it is also referred to colloquially as one of Fuller's follies after an eccentric local man, John "Mad Jack" Fuller (see p. 160), known for several other follies in the area.

He is said to have had this one built one night to win a drunken bet. Fuller bargained he could see the spire of Dallington Church from his house, Rose Hill, in Brightling. As the story goes, being unable to see the spire of the church, he organised for the sugarloaf to be built quickly to replicate it.

Mad Jack is said to have lived life to the full, revelling in his nickname to enhance his eccentric image. He was a member of the Fuller family who were wealthy local landowners at Brightling in East Sussex from the late 16th century onwards: their fortune was built upon iron and the manufacture of iron goods, especially cannons and similar equipment for the British Royal Navy. They also derived a substantial income from sugar plantations in Jamaica.

# JOHN "MAD JACK" FULLER'S MAUSOLEUM

⑩

## *A nod to the ancient Egyptians*

*St Thomas a Becket churchyard*
*Brightling, East Sussex, TN32 5HE*
*Daily 9am–5pm*

Brightling is a tiny blink-and-you'll-miss-it East Sussex village, home to an odd sight you cannot overlook: a giant tomb shaped like a pyramid.

This 7.6-metre-high Grade II listed mausoleum was built in 1811 by an eccentric wealthy local man called John "Mad Jack" Fuller. He built it 23 years before his death.

Fuller came from a wealthy family who made money from the iron industry and later from owning sugar plantations in Jamaica. He inherited Rose Hill, the family mansion in Brightling, in 1777 at the age of 20, along with a vast fortune. He is known for his eccentric personality and varied career: he was a squire, a Member of Parliament, a captain in the Sussex Militia, a Lieutenant Colonel in the Sussex Yeomanry Cavalry, a philanthropist, a patron of the arts and the sciences, and a public benefactor of the Belle Tout lighthouse at East Dean and other local amenities.

However, he is best known now for the many follies he built around his estate after his retirement from politics, possibly to relieve unemployment in the area – these include the Sugarloaf in Dallington (see p. 158).

You cannot go inside the pyramid, but a sign on the gated entrance of the mausoleum provides a fun distraction from this. It encourages visitors to peek through the grille for a glimpse of Mad Jack Fuller in full dress and top hat seated at a table set with a roast chicken and a bottle of wine. It is an endearing local legend, which has seen several versions told over the years, even though it is known that Fuller is buried in the conventional manner, in the ground, underneath the mausoleum.

The tomb was designed by an architect called Robert Smirke. At the time, Smirke had recently returned from a trip to Italy, and was inspired by the design of the Pyramid of Cestius in Rome.

Today, Smirke's tomb looks much as it did when it was built, albeit a little more weather-worn and moss-covered, which only adds to its quirky, macabre appeal.

In 1987, cracks began to appear at the base of the pyramid and the structure looked as though it was slipping. Concerned local supporters of the quirky grave set up a fund which paid for the foundations to be checked, and the mausoleum was repaired.

## *Another tomb in a pyramid*

John "Mad Jack" Fuller was not the only Sussex worthy to be entombed in a pyramid. London builder James Burton (1761–1837), credited with creating the town of St Leonards near Hastings in East Sussex between 1827 and 1837, is buried inside a similar construction, together with other family members. It can be found on West Hill Road in St Leonards, overlooking the sea.

# LITTLE ROAR GILL

⑪

## *A lost waterfall in a unique hidden valley*

*Old Roar Gill and Coronation Wood Nature Reserve*
*Alexandra Park, St Helen's Road, Hastings, East Sussex, TN37 7HF*

Alexandra Park in the north of Hastings in East Sussex hides a secret which so many residents do not know about, or if they do, they have not ventured to it yet.

If you head into the northern part of the park, you will find a unique nature reserve called Old Roar Gill which is home to an ancient waterfall called Little Roar Gill that, until recently, lay neglected and overlooked since the great storm of 1987.

The waterfall reopened in 2013 after a massive regeneration project led by Sussex Wildlife Trust and Hastings Borough Council. To mark this occasion, local volunteers staged a night-time walk from Alexandra Park to Old Roar Gill Local Nature Reserve, where Little Roar Gill was specially lit for the occasion with burning torches.

Old Roar Gill nature reserve is a hidden treasure in itself: a walk through it to discover the waterfall makes for an other-worldly experience. It occupies a pretty setting in a deeply cut, narrow wooded valley which runs along the upper reaches of a stream, which rises on a sandstone ridge to the north of Hastings and eventually runs into the sea.

Being in the reserve feels like you are in a rainforest, not in the middle of a residential area of a Sussex town: it is rich in ferns and moss and home to rare orchids. In spring, it is carpeted in ancient woodland flowers, such as bluebells, wood anemone and avens.

To find this curious waterfall, take the pathway through Alexandra Park that follows the stream under the road bridge to the wall. You can also get to it if you drive up Ghyllside Avenue: you will find an alleyway to the left which takes you down to a stream. If you follow the footpath through the reserve, it takes you past several mini falls on the way.

The lower section of Old Roar Gill and the land that is now Coronation Wood was bought by Hastings Borough Council between 1930 and 1935. In 1995 the upper section was purchased too. The whole area was declared a Local Nature Reserve in 2002 with the support of English Nature.

A chalk and graphite sketch of Little Roar Gill by William Turner dating back to 1806 can be found in the Tate Britain Prints and Drawings Room archives which can be viewed by appointment. The collection includes other sketches he did of Hastings: Ore Place, views above the town and Hastings Castle, to name but a few.

# AMSTERDAM SHIPWRECK

⑫

## *The outline of a perfectly preserved shipwreck*

*Bulverhythe Beach, Hastings, East Sussex*
*Open to view several times a year at very low tide*

A few times a year on the beach at Bulverhythe just west of Hastings, at very low tide, timbers marking the outline of the hull of a giant wrecked cargo ship are visible.

The *Amsterdam* is unique worldwide in that almost two-thirds of it is perfectly preserved beneath the surface. The nature of the muddy claylike sand on Bulverhythe beach – often described as quicksand – where the ship ran aground, meant that within a few months the hull had sunk over 8 metres into the silt, protecting it. It was not long before it was completely submerged and had disappeared from view, along with its cargo of treasures.

The wreck was not rediscovered until 1969, when it was exposed by a low spring tide. During a normal low tide, all that can be seen of the vessel is the top of the timbers sticking out of the clay beach. It is fascinating to see the outline of the top of the hull and imagine the historic, treasure-packed vessel preserved below.

The *Amsterdam* belonged to the East India Trading Company and ran aground here on 26 January 1749 after encountering a severe storm in the English Channel. It was on the return leg of its maiden voyage between the Netherlands and Java in Indonesia when it hit trouble. At the time, it was loaded up with goods and all kinds of treasures, like textiles, wine, cannon – as well as 30 chests filled with silver bullion.

It had been a difficult voyage from start to finish. Fifty members of the 333-strong crew had died of plague, while 40 more people are said to have been sick and dying when it beached. The trouble did not end there, however – it is said that smugglers and Hastings locals raided the ship of its silver cargo and wine, which led to one man being shot dead when fighting broke out after they got drunk.

## *A guided walk around the wreck*

Volunteers from the Shipwreck Museum in Hastings run anecdote-packed guided walks around the *Amsterdam* wreck at various times during the year. They also offer tours of another wreck found at nearby Pett Level, a 17th-century warship called *Anne*, which can be seen at extremely low spring tide, but only when the sands have moved from over the wreck. For more details, visit their website at shipwreckmuseum.co.uk, email info@shipwreckmuseum.co.uk or call 01424 437452.

# BOTTLE ALLEY LIGHT SHOW

(13)

## *Local colour*

*The Promenade*
*St Margaret's Road, Saint Leonards-on-Sea, East Sussex, TN37 6BZ*
*Daily at 7.30pm and 9.30pm for 10 minutes, and 30 minutes on Friday evenings*

An alternative to walking along Hastings' seafront next to the busy A259 is to make a detour down to the sheltered lower-deck promenade. It is known as Bottle Alley and it runs 455 metres from Warrior Square in St Leonards to Hastings pier.

It is an incredible feat of engineering made from 42,000 tonnes of concrete that 100 men a day built over six months. Opened in 1934, people soon started referring to it as Bottle Alley because of all the little pieces of broken glass embedded into the concrete wall panels that line the entire walkway.

On rainy days, it is the perfect spot for a seafront stroll away from the elements. Unless the weather is pleasant, though, it can feel a bit like walking through a damp and soulless concrete tunnel.

In the evening, however, the space is transformed when it becomes the setting for an atmospheric light show, known as the Bottle Alley Light Show, which takes place twice a night.

Walking through the tunnel as the colours change is a mesmerising experience, stopping people in their tracks to take in the details.

It was installed in 2017 to replace the old strip lighting and can produce all kinds of effects, from those resembling a subtle wave to a riot of colour. Looking back at it from the pier and seeing the whole tunnel lit up gives a sense of the light show as a whole.

This lower promenade was built as part of a revolutionary double-deck promenade in the 1930s by the borough engineer Sidney Little, who became known as the "concrete king". It was originally built as an undercover walkway for people to use to escape the bad weather and once had shutters. Although these shutters are no longer in place, the tracks can still be seen.

Information boards added after a recent revamp of Bottle Alley tell the story of the promenade's construction between October 1933 and April 1934, and include some eye-opening snippets. For example, 15 tonnes of broken glass pieces were set into 320 concrete panels made from 4,360 tonnes of concrete.

Further along the promenade towards Hastings pier is the entrance to the old White Rock Baths under the promenade, originally built in the late 1800s. They were revamped by "concrete king" Sydney Little in the 1930s into a complex including an ice rink, swimming pool and Turkish baths. Today it is an underground skate park (see p. 168).

# SOURCE PARK

14

## *The world's largest subterranean skate park*

*White Rock*
*Hastings, East Sussex, TN34 1JL*
*01424 460943*
*sourcebmx.com/pages/sourcepark*
*Daily 12noon–10pm, sometimes open earlier at weekends and in school holidays*

Hidden underneath the main promenade on Hastings' seafront, Source Park is a giant skateboarding and BMX complex that features two skate areas, a café, a shop, and room for 600 spectators across two balconies overlooking the main arena.

Despite its size, its underground location means you would hardly realise it is there, unless you are into skating and BMXing and know what you are looking for. It remains so well hidden that many people just walk past without noticing it.

Source Park is set in the former White Rock Baths, an old Victorian swimming complex built in the late 1800s and refurbished by Sydney Little, known as the "concrete king", who built the whole of the front of Hastings, including the double-decker promenade known as Bottle Alley, which features a light show every night (see p. 166).

Source Park was set up by Richard and Marc Moore, passionate local skaters with a clear vision: create the world's biggest underground skatepark. Making their dream a reality involved an epic two-year renovation project peppered with innumerable pitfalls. They rose above the challenges and opened the skate park in 2016 on the same day as the anniversary of the Battle of Hastings, hosting an eponymously named skate competition which attracted the best in global skating.

"It still amazes me that this epic space hiding underground was there all this time, walking into this crazy space underground, hundreds of years old, pretty much under the sea", says Mark.

The old White Rocks Baths building has had several other uses since it was built, including as a Turkish bathhouse where people would come for hot seawater baths before a cigarette or two in the smoking room, which is now the new Source shop. It has also been used as a cinema, a swimming pool and an ice rink.

An award-wining film called *The Source Park: Bringing the White Rock Back to Life* documents the transformation of the old swimming baths into the skate park. It tells the story of Hastings' skate scene and another skate park which opened in the same location in 1977. It was called the Concrete Cave and is thought to have been immediately popular, attracting loads of local skaters – including a member of the Dogtown skate team.

You can read about the documentary on the Source Park blog or buy it from the Source Park shop.

# TRUE CRIME MUSEUM

15

## *Morbidly fascinating*

*Palace Avenue Arcade*
*White Rock, Hastings, East Sussex, TN34 1JP*
*01424 420115*
*truecrimemuseum.co.uk*
*Daily 10am–5pm*

Set in a series of caves underneath the former Palace Court Hotel building is a bizarre museum filled with "murderabilia". That is, memorabilia and forensic evidence relating to murders and violent events.

The growing collection is vast, covering all aspects of true crime: from the Mafia, drug lords and serial killers, to football hooliganism and armed robbery. For an hour or more, you will be totally gripped, surprised, sickened and morbidly fascinated in equal measure, at every turn.

Visitors are eased in with the gruesome, yet familiar story of Jack the Ripper on a timeline peppered with facts and anecdotes relating to the Victorian era. Turn the corner, though, and you are met with the sight of a real electric chair, which you can sit in and pretend you are next for the chop.

A fascinating story is told in every cabinet. There is one filled with homemade weapons confiscated from Bangu Tres in Rio de Janeiro, one of the world's most dangerous prisons. In another is a Victorian bodice, belonging to Amelia Dyer, a baby farmer, who adopted orphaned children for money before murdering them. In one corner, a bullet-riddled car (pictured) tells the story of the Mexican cocaine king Heriberto Lazcano.

Slightly less stomach-churning is a cabinet filled with recognisable items like a packet of cigarettes, a £10 note, and a bottle of Chanel Number 5 perfume – but can you tell whether they are real or fake?

Elsewhere, in the "death chamber" is a real lethal injection bed, complete with a description of how the system works. If your nerves can take it, a short film in the screening room shows actual serial killers discussing the murders they carried out.

This bizarre, but brilliant collection of murder-related memorabilia is curated by collector Joel Griggs, who became interested in murderabilia aged eight when he witnessed a bank robbery carried out by a man called John Childs, who later became one of the UK's most prolific contract killers. Childs killed six people and cut up the bodies into tiny pieces in his bath, before burning them in his fireplace.

"He lived four doors down from my great uncle in Poplar, London, who worked for the council's civic amenity department", he says. "They cleared Childs' flat and took the bath to the Poplar refuse depot, where it was planted in a garden of remembrance. When the depot closed down, my uncle took the bath to his allotment in Walthamstow, where he used it as a water trough. Now, it's in the museum!"

# FLOWER MAKERS' MUSEUM

(16)

## *A pseudo florist*

*Shirley Leaf and Petal Co*
*58a High Street, Hastings, East Sussex, TN34 3EN*
*01424 427793*
*martin-enterprises.eu/leafmuseum.html*
*Monday to Saturday 10am–4pm*

At first glance, the setting for the intriguing Flower Makers' Museum might look like an ordinary high street florist. Close up, you will see that the flowers decorating the front window and spilling out the door are in fact artificial.

This is the headquarters of a curious business known as the Shirley Leaf and Petal Co, a company which specialises in making artificial flowers, petals, leaves and foliage for film and television shows, film production companies, theatre shows and fashion houses.

Established in east London in the 19th century, it moved to Hastings in 1910: its beautiful old shopfront is a clue that it has been here a while.

Filled with faux flowers and foliage galore, the shop is a gem in itself, but hiding in its basement is a most fascinating discovery called the Flower Makers' Museum – a little-known working collection consisting of everything involved in manufacturing fake flowers and foliage. You are free to browse unaccompanied and touch anything within reach.

The museum was set up in 1981 by the present owner, Brenda, who moved all the company's machinery and stock from storage to the present location when she bought the company.

The collection starts on the stairs, crowded with displays and stock, leading down to two rooms in the basement. One contains a large press behind glass and a huge collection of thousands of cutting tools on shelves. The other is loosely organised into sections – one area looks like an old factory office dating back to around 1910, with ledgers and historic health and safety notices. Another is devoted to clothes and other things decorated with the flowers.

Every bit of space is filled. There are bales of silk and other fabric, and boxes of supplies. Small cardboard mounted displays can be leafed through and contain samples, ephemera and correspondence relating to noteworthy film or theatre jobs.

One of the largest objects they have created for a performance is the "singing tree", made from over a million leaves and incorporating hidden seating for a choir. They have also made chiffon leaf trails for the English National Ballet, olive leaves for the *Oberammergau Passion Play*, leaves for the Disney film *Pocahontas*, trees for the Millennium Dome, dahlias for Glyndebourne Opera House and, most recently, petals for the Broadway production of *Frozen*.

# FAT TUESDAY

17

## *The biggest Mardi Gras festival outside New Orleans*

*Various venues around Hastings, East Sussex*
*hastingsfattuesday.co.uk*
*Open five days throughout February or March each year*
*Admission free*

Most of us are more likely to know Fat Tuesday as Shrove Tuesday – or better still, Pancake Day. Whatever you call it, and depending on your religion and where you live, it is traditionally a celebration and feast day before Ash Wednesday, the first day of Lent – a time of fasting which lasts for 40 days leading up to Easter.

In New Orleans and Rio de Janiero, it is celebrated with *Mardi Gras*, while in Venice it is called *Carnivale*. Now in the UK, as well as flipping pancakes, we have the chance to celebrate this day of the year musically at the Fat Tuesday festival – which is simply the English translation of the French term Mardi Gras ("Mardi" meaning "Tuesday", and "Gras" meaning "fat").

In the name of tradition, the Fat Tuesday festival takes place each year as close to Shrove Tuesday as possible. It sees over 250 free gigs taking place across 30 different venues around Hastings – from the First In Last Out and The Crown, to the Stade Hall and the White Rock Hotel, to name but a few, showcasing the town's thriving music scene. Despite the event's stature, it still remains unknown to most Sussex residents, unless you live or have friends and family in Hastings, or are seriously into music and follow the festival scene meticulously.

Fat Tuesday was established in 2009 by musician Bob Tipler and event organiser Adam Daly. Since its early days, it has grown considerably and become the launch event for the area-wide Music Month initiative, which runs from Valentine's Day to St Patrick's Day and celebrates local music. It has also been described as Hastings' answer to the South by Southwest (SXSW) festival in Texas, and compared with Brighton's Great Escape festival, similar in that gigs take place at different venues around town. Fat Tuesday has since grown into a key event in the Hastings cultural calendar, which in 2018 saw an audience of 14,000.

As well as a packed gig timetable, the programme includes other events such as curated performances, family activities, the Umbrella Parade, Le Grand Mardi Gras Ball, Sonics, a two-day celebration of experimental and electronic music and visuals, and a day-long music-industry event called UnConvention.

# AG HENDY HOUSE

(18)

*Like stepping into a Brothers Grimm fairytale*

*135 All Saints Street*
*Hastings, East Sussex, TN34 3BG*
*01424 447171*
*aghendy.com/house*
*info@aghendy.com*
*Open for tours by appointment – see the website for details*

All Saints Street in Hastings' Old Town is lined with chocolate box cottages, but none more intriguing than number 135. With its weathered Tudor façade and giant Caucasian Hogweed, it has a fairy-tale quality which makes you want to peek inside. You can do this on atmospheric tours, some of which take place by candlelight.

The Grade II-listed 16th-century merchant house is owned by Alastair Hendy, a food writer and photographer who also owns the fascinating AG Hendy & Co homewares shop not far from here, at 36 High Street. When he bought the house in 2006, it did not look anything like it does now and he did not know what he was going to do with it.

"Everything inside was modern, even the Tudor front had been covered up", he says. "I wanted to restore it, but never had in mind the vision of the house as it now is. I just looked over the property and this obsession gradually took hold of me."

Rather than try to recreate a Tudor house of the time, he has restored it to bring out its character, with the "AG Hendy touch", which took five years. "I made the structure solid and restored every surface, obsessing over every tiny detail."

The result is this intriguing time-capsule home which you can visit on a tour at various time of year. Inside, it feels as if you have walked into the pages of a Brothers Grimm fairy-tale book.

There are four upper rooms, above a front parlour and middle parlour kitchen, a double-height rear wing where you will find the kitchen and a dining room in a semi-underground cellar. There is also a little back yard with an outdoor toilet and shower set in a replica fish smokehouse. The furniture is an eclectic mix of European pieces from all periods: 19th-century Orkney chairs with rush backs that sit alongside English Georgian wingbacks in velvet and an 18th-century West Country settle with its original paint.

"Tours take about an hour, and I try to make them relaxed and informal. I'll talk a bit about things and leave people to look around on their own, rather than getting everyone to follow on in a big group. The rooms are too small for that anyway", he says.

"People are welcome to find me if they have questions. I don't want things to be stuffy".

At Christmas, the tours are run by candlelight, which is magical.

It is even possible to stay for a night or two.

# RYE TOWN MODEL SOUND AND LIGHT SHOW

(19)

*Murder, mystery and mayhem*

*Rye Heritage Centre*
*Strand Quay, The Old Sail Loft, Rye, East Sussex, TN31 7AY*
*01797 226696*
*ryeheritage.co.uk*
*Daily 10am–5pm in summer, 10am–4pm in winter*
*Showings every 20 minutes, or on demand by prior booking throughout the day*
*Last show 20 minutes before closing time*

Set in a purpose-built theatre hidden inside the Rye Heritage Centre is this quirky experience which offers visitors a more novel way to appreciate the town of Rye on the East Sussex coast. It brings 700 years of Rye's history to life, giving context to many of the town's main tourist sights.

The experience starts by giving the audience a sense of direction, pointing out the old town wall and various landmarks within the town walls. It then tells stories chosen by its creators, local couple Joy and Ted Harland, to reflect the more dramatic episodes of Rye's illustrious history – from its early days as a coastal Cinque Port to a smuggling base in the 18th century, via French raids, monastic intrigue, two royal visits and a notorious local murder, carried out by John "Butcher" Breads.

His skull is said to be stored away in the attic of the town hall, along with the gibbet cage he was executed in, which can be viewed by arrangement with Rye Town Council (see p. 182).

As the stories unfold, the commentary is enhanced by dramatic sound and light effects.

Although the model looks as though it could be brand new, Joy built the model between 1973 and 1976. A retired teacher and keen amateur artist, she was inspired by Son et Lumiere (sound and light) shows she had seen after travelling in France and Belgium to create an educational and entertaining equivalent for Rye.

Set against a backdrop painting of the surrounding countryside by local artist John Izod, the model shows the town not as it is today, but rather as it was over a century ago in 1872, a time at which Joy considered Rye to be at its most beautiful architecturally.

Looking at it, you could be forgiven for thinking that little about Rye has changed. Although it has altered a lot in detail since 1872, the town plan has changed little, and Rye is believed to have retained more of its original historic buildings than any other town in Britain.

Joy created the model using a combination of written records, building surveys, aerial photographs, and the Ordnance Survey Map of the time, and spent three years producing each building to 1:100 scale.

The lights were added by her husband, Ted, a retired electrical engineer, who spent six months wiring them in and creating the original audio track once the model was complete.

With this in mind, head upstairs to the first floor for some light relief. Up here you will find one of the UK's largest collections of working antique models and novelty games from British seaside piers and amusement arcades. The Old Pier Penny Arcade is made up of over 30 restored, fully operational machines from the early 1900s to 1960, and includes the famous Sidney Knows fortune teller, The Laughing Sailor, and The Haunted Churchyard.

# RYE WATER HOUSE

20

## *A novel miniature home or glorified cistern?*

*3 Church Square, Rye, East Sussex, TN31 7HE*
*Open to view from the outside only*

Near the grounds of St Mary's Churchyard – in a part of Rye once known as Pump Street – the Rye Water House is a bizarre oval-shaped building set on top of a dome structure.

With two little white doors on either side, at first glance it is easy to assume that it is a novel miniature dwelling, until you discover the plaque on the wall in front which reveals you are in fact looking at a water cistern built between 1733 and 1735, as part of a plan to improve the town's water system.

Locally, it is known as the Rye Water House, and it once formed an important part of the water supply system in the 18th century. Water was piped into the town from the north-east to a water house on Cinque Ports Street. From this water house, it was pumped using a horse gin along an elm pipe up Conduit Hill to the cistern we see here.

It was located here as it was the highest point in the town and could hold about 20,000 gallons, which were distributed through wooden pipes to properties in the upper parts of Rye.

At the time it was built, the area around the water house was used for butchery. A lack of hygienic practices among the butchery businesses nearby led to unsavoury discoveries of calves' feet in the reservoir. Recognising the health risk, it became a criminal offence to litter anywhere near the Rye Water House.

## NEARBY

### *The Waterworks: from pump house to microbrewery*

*The Waterworks, Tower Street, Rye, East Sussex, TN31 7ET*
*01797 224110*
*ryewaterworks.co.uk*

Not far from the Rye Water House is another curious building that once played a part in Rye's water system. The "Water Works" was once a pumping station built in 1869 and reopened in 1907 as a soup kitchen, several old features from which time have been preserved. These include large fireplaces and bases which once housed large copper soup vats. Today, it is home to the first micropub in East Sussex: The Rye Waterworks serves eight local ales.

# REMAINS OF JOHN "BUTCHER" BREADS ㉑

## *The extraordinary story of the murderer in the Rye*

*Rye Town Council*
*Town Hall, Market Street, Rye, East Sussex, TN31 7LA*
*ryetowncouncil.gov.uk*
*01797 223902*
*Open to see by appointment only*

The attic of the Rye Town Council offices is the unlikely setting for what looks like an instrument of torture: a body-shaped cage containing the skull of a notorious local murderer.

John Breads was a local butcher with a history of violence, having already appeared in court charged with stabbing a man in the arm. He was later executed in 1743 for murdering a man called Allen Grebell, whom he mistook for his intended victim, James Lamb, the Mayor of Rye at the time.

Breads was angry that Lamb had convicted him of using false weights to sell his meat. Several of his drinking pals at his local pub, the Flushing Inn, witnessed him swearing his revenge.

The story goes that Breads planned to ambush Lamb in the churchyard on the way home from a party he was due to attend. Unbeknown to Breads, Lamb became ill, so Lamb's brother-in-law, Allen Grebell, went to the party in his place wearing Lamb's coat. Mistaking Grebell for Lamb, Breads stabbed him a number of times including two fatal blows to his lungs, before throwing his engraved knife into the bushes and escaping.

Miraculously, Grebell made it home, told his servant he had been attacked and slumped into a chair. His servant, believing him drunk, went to bed, only to discover him dead in a pool of blood in the morning.

John "Butcher" Breads was caught, imprisoned in the Ypres Tower, hanged shortly after and his body gibbetted in the cage; that is, it was left to rot for more than 20 years in the cage on public display on Gibbet Marsh, across the river from Rye Windmill, now home to a car park.

According to reports, on the day of his death, the executioner collected Breads from his cell and took him to his place of execution on the marsh, stopping briefly at the murderer's favourite pub, the Flushing Inn, so that the condemned man could have one last drink.

The gruesome story of John "Butcher" Breads features as part of the Rye Town Model Show, a quirky, alternative audio tour of the town's history. See p. 178.

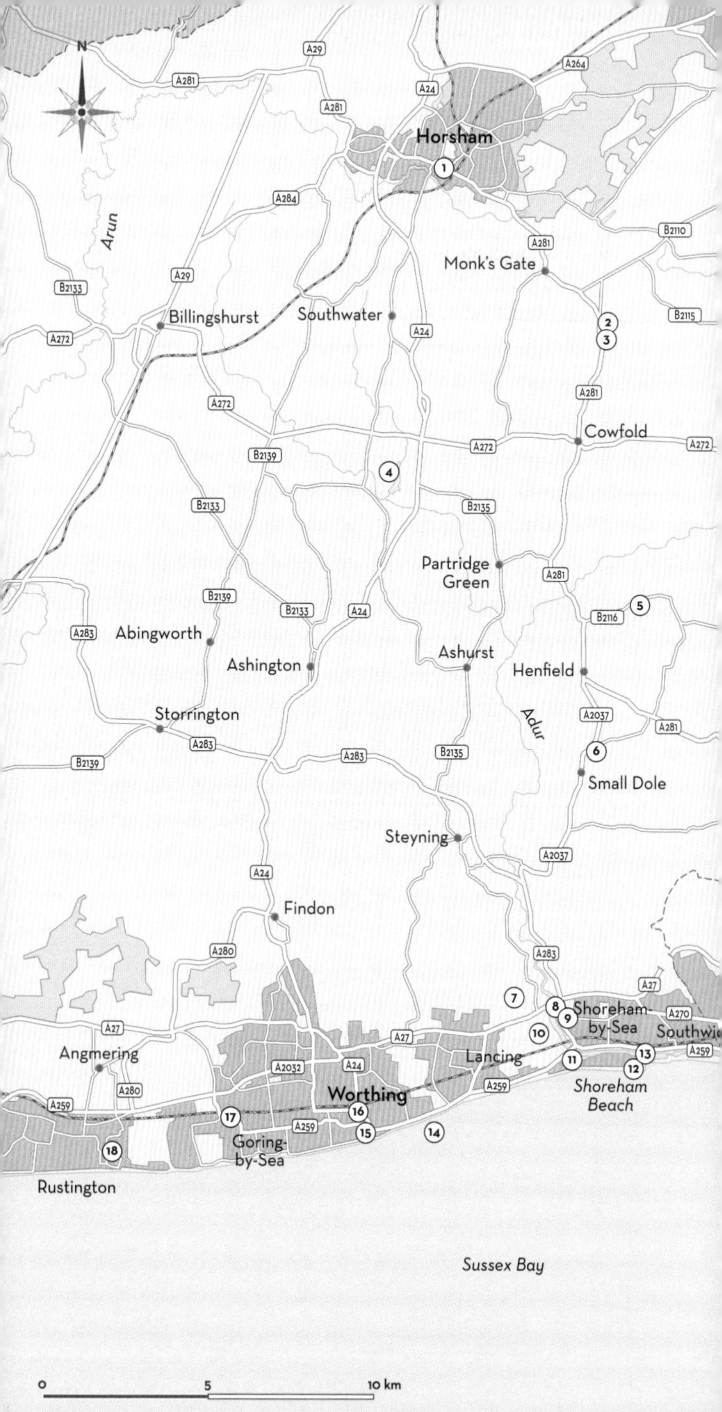
N
Horsham
Monk's Gate
Billingshurst
Southwater
Arun
Cowfold
Partridge Green
Abingworth
Ashington
Ashurst
Henfield
Storrington
Adur
Small Dole
Steyning
Findon
Shoreham-by-Sea
Southwick
Lancing
Angmering
Worthing
Goring-by-Sea
Shoreham Beach
Rustington
Sussex Bay
A29
A281
A264
A24
A284
B2110
B2133
B2115
A272
A281
B2139
B2135
A283
B2116
A2037
A280
A27
A270
A259
A2032
1
2
3
4
5
6
7
8
9
10
11
12
13
14
15
16
17
18
0
5
10 km

# *Horsham to Worthing*

# WILLIAMS & CO PHARMACY

①

## *Remnants of a Victorian high street shop*

*The Horsham Museum & Art Gallery*
*9 Causeway, Horsham, West Sussex, RH12 1HE*
*01403 254959*
*horshammuseum.org*
*Monday to Saturday 10am–5pm*

Old shops are having a moment right now: entire social media accounts and websites exist purely to document their shopfronts and ghost signs. New shops and restaurants are often designed to look old-fashioned. We also love buying vinyl, wearing vintage clothing, watching old programmes and going on throwback nights out.

The deceptively cavernous Horsham Museum, a hidden Sussex gem in itself, offers visitors the chance to satisfy this yearning for the past: it is filled to the brim with all kinds of nostalgic treasures relating to the town's retail history, and these can be found in the ground-floor Shopping Gallery.

The collection includes this gem of a shopfront which reflects the town's retail past – the fixtures and fittings of Williams & Co, a pharmacy dating back to 1870, once located at 21 West Street. The shopfront set-up is guaranteed to steal your gaze for hours, as you take in all the tiny details.

Original pieces include the Victorian drug drawers, the shop signage and an etched panel to the side of the shopfront. The drawers were still in use until the shop closed in the early 1970s; each one labelled with an abbreviated pharmaceutical term explained on a sheet on the counter. The etched glass window reflects the Victorian love affair with ornamentation.

The cabinet beneath the counter is filled with a mesmerising collection of old pharmacy bottles, tins, scales and other equipment. The adding machine, which looks like a cash register, is a museum piece in itself, dating back to the late 1800s. A nearby cabinet houses an impressive collection of carved gingerbread moulds, relating to Horsham's history as the centre for this sweet treat.

Elsewhere, the costume gallery upstairs offers an exciting collection of shoes dating from 1670 to 2000, as well as accessories like hats, hat pins, costume jewellery, ethnographic jewellery, chatelaines, purses and handbags. Everything is stored in a set of beautiful old drawers from a 1950s ladies' outfitters. It is fun to open each one to discover what is inside.

Cabinets of curiosity, also known as wonder rooms, get a mention on this floor, too. These were usually small personal collections, which like today's museums, attempted to categorise and tell stories about the wonders and oddities of the natural world. The one at Horsham includes a narwhal horn thought at one time to come from a unicorn.

# DOLLS' HOUSE MUSEUM ②

## *It's a small world*

*Leonardslee Lakes and Gardens*
*Brighton Road, Lower Beeding, Horsham, West Sussex, RH13 6PP*
*0871 8733 389*
*leonardsleegardens.co.uk/dolls-house-museum*
*Daily 1 April to 31 October: 10–6pm, 1 November to 31 March: 10–4pm*
*Closed 25 December*

A mob of wallabies and a Michelin-starred restaurant are not the only surprises awaiting visitors to Leonardslee Lakes and Gardens in West Sussex (see p. 190 and p. 226). Tucked inside a little room next to the courtyard restaurant is an imaginary market town and country estate, created entirely in miniature.

This magical diminutive world was designed and created by hand by local artist Helen Holland. It depicts the story of life in an English country estate and a local market town in the early 1900s.

Holland was commissioned to create the collection in the Dolls' House Museum by the previous owner of Leonardslee, Christopher Loder, who liked a piece she had previously made for him so much, he commissioned this vast estate. Opened in 1999 after 10 years of work, it has since been expanded and recently restored.

The imaginary town and estate are made up of a variety of buildings and materials to reflect the fact a country estate evolves over many years. The attention to detail is incredible: you can easily spend an hour taking in all the tiny hand-painted features, thinking you have seen everything, but soon spotting plenty of others.

On the whole, it gives a clear sense of how an estate took shape in the form of a mansion, entrance lodge, farm buildings, granary, farm garden, topiary garden, kitchen garden, walled garden, keeper's cottage, gardener's cottage, and stable yard. These elements surround the edge of the room along with a church, school and churchyard.

There are also lots of shops, workshops and social gathering places to peer inside: a greengrocer's, butcher's, post office, laundry, wheelwright, carpenter and cabinet maker, church, pub, and school.

On closer inspection, you will notice that some of the figures are actually moving: there is a man sawing timber, another forging ironwork, a lady making a wedding dress and even a dance at the hay barn.

There are lots of other surprise things to look out for, too, such as a mouse under the trolley in the inn, the hedgehog making its escape from a bonfire, a boy in the front of the class wearing a dunce hat, to name but a few.

> Rumour has it a ghost has been spotted floating around the churchyard ...

# LEONARDSLEE WALLABIES

③

## *A secret mob*

*Leonardslee Gardens*
*Brighton Road, Lower Beeding, Horsham, East Sussex, RH13 6PP*
*0871 873 3389*
*leonardsleegardens.co.uk*
*Daily 10am–6pm in spring/summer, 10am–4pm in autumn/winter*

Leonardslee Lakes and Gardens near the market town of Horsham is home to two distinguishing features. The first is the incredible world created entirely in miniature found inside the Dolls' House Museum (see p. 188). The second is a colony of wallabies, some of them albino, who are the descendants of the original animals brought here in 1889 by the previous owner of Leonardslee Lakes and Gardens, Sir Edmund Loder.

Loder is often described as an eccentric naturalist, of which there were many in the Victorian era.

The wallabies have roamed the estate ever since and are thought to be Bennett's wallabies – also better-known as red-necked wallabies. They are a species native to the Australian island of Tasmania. Their thick coats make them able to withstand the British weather, which is why Loder and other naturalists at the time chose to import them.

Other colonies can be found in Scotland, the Isle of Man, Lambay

Island off the east coast of Ireland and the Peak District in Staffordshire.

There are two ways to see the wallabies at Leonardslee. For a guaranteed glimpse, you will find around 10 or so wallabies hopping around inside an enclosure known as the Wallaby Park, tucked behind the main house. This is where breeding pairs are kept, and anyone is free to visit at any time of year.

Outside the enclosure, there is thought to be an unknown number of wallabies living semi-wild across the estate within gated areas. These are often spotted around the lakes and mostly in the middle section of the gardens. Random sightings in the local area have even been reported by surprised residents.

The breeding pairs are entertaining to watch, especially in early spring when mothers carry their babies in their pouches, and in May and June when the babies start learning to walk around. In summer, males perform boxing-style bouts with each other as a way of competing for mates.

This colony of wallabies and their Australian bushland heritage inspired the new Australia Garden at Leonardslee.

The garden was designed by the landscape architect John Write, who lived in Australia as a development officer for the University of Tasmania. It features lots of eucalyptus trees with their open canopies, ferns and lots of lush low-lying plants. Elsewhere, Leonardslee is a treasure trove of rare and unusual specimens, with around 10 champion trees and huge magnolias collected by Sir Edmund Loder in the 19th century.

# KNEPP WILDLAND

④

*The setting for a pioneering conservation project*

*Knepp Castle Estate*
*West Grinstead, Horsham, West Sussex, RH13 8LJ*
*01403 713230*
*knepp.co.uk*
*Open all year round*
*Download a walking map from a link here: knepp.co.uk/contact*

Set on 3,500 acres, south of Horsham in West Sussex, the Knepp Castle Estate is an English country manor house property with a distinguishing feature. Its surrounding landscape looks more like the wild and dynamic African bushland than traditional English countryside.

Footpaths through the estate are left open all year round to encourage curious visitors to explore these intriguing surroundings. Encounters with herds of wild ponies, cattle, deer and pigs as they roam are almost always guaranteed, not to mention sightings of once-rare birds, mammals, butterflies, beetles, reptiles, plants and fungi.

This wild landscape is the result of a conservation project called Knepp Wildland, which uses a process known as "rewilding" to encourage and maintain diversity. Until 2001, most of this land was used for traditional arable and dairy farming, until the owners Sir Charles Burrell and his author and travel writer wife, Isabella Tree, started taking a hands-off approach to conservation.

The aim of rewilding is to establish an ecosystem where nature is given as much freedom as possible, rather than employing those set out in traditional conservation projects which have specific goals for specific species.

"What we've done here? We've taken a step back and taken our hands off the steering wheel and let nature take over, and of course wonderful things have started happening", says Tree in a film made in conjunction with the project.

Turtle doves, nightingales, peregrine falcons and purple emperor butterflies have been seen breeding here. And populations of more common species are rocketing. The Barbastelle bat, probably Europe's most rare mammal, has also been seen, not to mention 26 species of beetle, as well as five owl species.

Farming is still practised at Knepp, just in a less intensive way, producing organic, pasture-fed meat from free-roaming herds of animals you can see within the wildland project.

## *Knepp Safaris*

A fun way to learn more about the estate's unique landscape, the rewilding project and its animals, is on a vehicle-based safari trip or a guided walking tour. There is also the opportunity to make a holiday out of it with a stay in one of the estate's treehouses, shepherd's huts, tents or yurts, or pitch your own tent in the wildland campsite. Visit kneppsafaris.co.uk, email safaris@knepp.co.uk or call 01403 713230.

# SUSSEX PRAIRIE GARDEN

⑤

## *Taming the wild*

*Morlands Farm*
*Wheatsheaf Road, Henfield, West Sussex, BN5 9AT*
*01273 495902*
*sussexprairies.co.uk*
*June to September: Wednesday to Monday 1pm–5pm*

Set on eight acres surrounded by oak trees, the hills of the High Weald undulating in the distance, the Sussex Prairie Garden is a miniature prairie-style garden that transports us to the golden wheat-filled plains of North America. It is the innovative work of garden designers Pauline and Paul McBride.

Creating a garden people would pay to visit had been a long-term dream for the couple, and it was finally realised when family business drew them back to the area. They spent three months drawing up detailed planting plans, and propagated every one of the 30,000 plants needed to fill the site. They started in 2008 with just a field and planted it in a fortnight: some people did the gardening while others did the cooking. They sold their first ticket to the Sussex Prairie Garden a year after it was planted.

The result is a free-flowing, naturalistic garden set out in a spiralling shell shape, the tearoom at one end, a field of sheep at the other.

Wide beds filled with vast clumps of tawny grasses sit between broad sweeping lawn paths. Plants are set out in bold groups for high impact and flower colours are generally quite soft and muted. The grasses grow so tall in summer that they tower over the paths.

The garden is inspired by the work of the grand master of prairie planting, Piet Oudolf, known for his off-beat approach to gardening and his naturalistic perennial meadow designs. He made his name designing the High Line in New York, an urban wilderness on a section of an abandoned elevated railway. He has also worked on the meadows at Hauser & Wirth's art gallery in Somerset, and the Olympic Park in Stratford, to name but a few.

The McBrides have been advocates of this form since they worked with Oudolf early in their garden designing careers, helping him implement a scheme he designed for a private estate in Luxembourg.

Oudolf chooses plants for their forms and textures rather than their flowers or decorative features, and also for the rhythm they create over the seasons. They look as good in decay as they do in the first unfurling of spring. So popular is his style, it is found all over: in local pocket parks, on roundabouts and in amenity schemes and now in Sussex. It has even sparked the "New Perennial" movement of which Oudolf is considered the spearhead.

# THE GREEN KNIGHT OF WOODS MILL

⑥

## *A mysterious mossy hidden grave*

*Woods Mill Nature Reserve*
*Shoreham Road, Henfield, East Sussex, BN5 9SD*
*sussexwildlifetrust.org.uk/visit/woods-mill*

The headquarters of the Sussex Wildlife Trust, Woods Mill Nature Reserve is a hidden gem in itself: it is a peaceful sanctuary and the setting for bird watching, nature spotting and pond dipping. It is also home to a bizarre grave shrouded in mystery.

To find it, head past the pop-up café inside the little caravan, and the pond, then over Hoe Bridge, until you see a path strewn either side with large, ornate stones and pieces of masonry covered in moss.

The grave is close to here, hidden amid the trees just off the path.

The origins of the mossy grave and the stones are a bit of a mystery. "We think the stones were imported here in the 1920s to be used as part of a folly when Woods Mill was run as tea rooms", says reserve manager, Steve Tillman. "We also think they might have come from the parliament building clear up – surplus stones from which that look similar to those at Woods Mill are advertised in an auction booklet from the early 20th century. Although they look medieval, they're more than likely Victorian", he adds.

The fact they were not used is linked to a scandal involving a previous Woods Mill owner, Arthur Peake from Brighton. In 1936, he was sentenced to death for murdering 22-year-old Arthur Noyce, his chauffeur – and likely lover – who is thought to be buried in the green knight's grave.

As well as this fascinating tale of scandal and intrigue, Woods Mill is an example of ancient woodland, with old ponds and a lake, streams and waterways to explore, and unimproved meadows with their wild hedgerows – habitats all contained within its 47 acres. This variety of habitat attracts an impressive number of species including mammals, insects, amphibians and birds.

It was also an important flour mill for the surrounding area, and records show that a mill has stood here since the Norman Conquest.

Visitors can still see the Victorian waterwheel and Old Miller's House which now provide a base for the staff. Water still plays a vital part in the wildlife diversity of the site: water shrews can sometimes be seen swimming from bank to bank, and the elusive water rail can be heard, and sometimes seen, tiptoeing along the bank edges. The streams are lined with blackthorn, hawthorn, greengage, willow and other trees, which are alive with birds in the spring and summer: bullfinch, blackcap, garden warbler, willow warbler and chiffchaff, each competing to be heard.

# LANCING COLLEGE CHAPEL

⑦

*The largest school chapel in the world and a miniature Westminster Abbey*

*Lancing College*
*Lancing, East Sussex, BN15 0RW*
*01273 465949*
*lancingcollege.co.uk/chapel*
*Daily 10am–4pm except when used for college ceremonies*
*See website for details*

With its striking Gothic exterior, Lancing College Chapel, just north of Brighton City Airport (see p. 206), is a captivating sight on an otherwise ordinary car journey along the A27.

Few people driving past it, however, make the detour for a look inside, probably because it is a college chapel, and it is not obvious or widely publicised that it is open to the public, which it is.

Up close, it is just as imposing as it is from a distance. However, its incomplete west side entrance – with its unfinished brickwork, temporary doors and boarded over arches – is no preparation for what is to come. Stepping inside the elaborate 27-metre-high Gothic nave, with its incredible vaulted ceiling, it feels like you have discovered a smaller version of Westminster Abbey, albeit only a fraction less tall.

Its design is known as neo-Gothic, Victorian Gothic or Gothic Revival, in that it imitates a style popular in 13th-century England, but it also has French influences. Layout-wise, it follows a standard English Gothic plan, with a triforium, and a high clerestory.

As well as its sheer size and beauty, there are many details to take in. For example, the stalls, which are thought to come from Eton College chapel, are topped with canopies designed by St Pancras Station architect Sir George Gilbert Scott.

With a diameter of 10 metres, the spectacular stained-glass rose window at the west end of the nave is thought to be the largest of its

kind in Europe. It was designed by Stephen Dykes Bower and is made of 30,000 pieces of glass.

Bower (whose work can also be found inside Westminster Abbey) also designed the ornate ceiling in the west end entry vestibule, where there is another stained-glass window to discover, this time designed by Mel Howse to honour Archbishop Trevor Huddleston, a former pupil of Lancing who campaigned against apartheid in South Africa.

Dedicated in 1911, Lancing College Chapel was founded in 1868 by Nathanial Woodward who founded the college. It is considered to be the largest school chapel in the world, and also the fourth tallest ecclesiastical building in Britain. What is also incredible about this building is that it is made entirely out of local Sussex sandstone sourced from the nearby village of Scaynes Hill in West Sussex.

If you look closely you might spot a carving of a mouse somewhere in the chapel ...

# DOWNS LINK



## *An atmospheric traffic-free trail along a disused railway line*

*Between Shoreham-by-Sea, West Sussex and St Martha's Hill, Surrey*
*westsussex.gov.uk/leisure-recreation-and-community/walking-horse-riding-and-cycling/downs-link/*

On the fringes of Shoreham-by-Sea next to the River Adur (where you will find an atmospheric memorial sculpture, see p. 204) is the start – or end, depending on where you live – of an overlooked, long-distance walking, cycling and bridle trail that links the South Downs Way with the North Downs Way.

It runs from Shoreham-by-Sea in West Sussex to St Martha's Hill in Surrey, and crosses the South Downs and Coastal Plain, the Surrey Hills and the Low Weald.

It largely follows the route of two disused railway lines, abandoned since the 1960s.

What is incredible is that, at 59 km in length, it is largely free from traffic and is set mostly off-road apart from in one place.

There are various ways to tackle it: you can just dip in and out on a Sunday stroll, completing a stage at a time, or explore the entire trail in one go, on a weekend walk or a full-day's cycle.

Since the trains stopped running along the route in the 1960s, the embankments and cuttings have been left to become a green corridor for wildlife and people, connecting different habitats, banks of wildflowers, trees, hedges, woodlands, rivers, ponds and streams.

It is not unusual to see butterflies, such as fritillaries and admirals, fluttering around the sheltered woodland glades, or kingfishers in the rivers. You might even spot bats foraging and, on summer evenings, hear nightingales singing and even see glow worms.

If you like the idea of exploring a specific section at a time, West Sussex County Council has created a six-stage route guide to download from its website – see link opposite. Each stage route explores a different part of the Downs Link, is between 6 km and 11 km in length, and is accessible by public transport or by car.

Two of the stage routes are in Sussex: Stage Five is 7.7 km long and takes in the pretty villages of Henfield, Steyning and Bramber, as well as the ruins of Bramber Castle, a Norman fortress built in 1070 in the South Downs (see p. XxX). Stage Six is 6.6 km long: it takes you from Bramber, past Botolphs where the South Downs Way meets the Downs Link, to Shoreham-by-Sea. During this stage walk, you will also pass an old green railway carriage set in the goods yard of West Grinstead Old Station. The carriage has been turned into an information centre run by volunteers, who aim to open it most Sundays (generally 10am–4pm).

# SHOREHAM AIRSHOW DISASTER MEMORIAL ⑨

## *A peaceful place of remembrance*

*Shoreham Pedestrian Toll Bridge, eastern end*
*Shoreham-by-Sea, West Sussex*

In August 2015, 11 men lost their lives when a Hawker Hunter jet crashed onto the A27 during the Shoreham Airshow. The victims were: Maurice Abrahams, 76; Tony Brightwell, 53; Matthew Grimstone, Jacob Schilt and Daniele Polito, all 23; Matt Jones, 24; Graham Mallinson, 72; Mark Reeves, 53; Dylan Archer, 42; Richard Smith, 26, and Mark Trussler, 54, who all lived in Sussex.

In the aftermath of the disaster, the east bank of the River Adur by the Shoreham Pedestrian Toll Bridge became a focal point for mourners, who came to reflect and pay respects in their hundreds, piling the riverbank high with bunches of flowers.

Today, the victims are remembered by a sculpture set on the east bank overlooking the river, acting as a place of peace and reflection. The installation was created by Portslade-based husband and wife artists Jane Fordham and David Parfitt. Together, they spent two years designing and making it. Throughout the process, they worked in very close collaboration with the families of the victims.

Fordham and Parfitt wanted to create a piece that would not only be an attractive public artwork to fit the surroundings, but also act as a place of reflection for people to come and acknowledge grief.

The result is this moving four-metre-high sculpture set on a beautiful hand-built mosaic next to a bench, which is facing it. It is made of 11 stainless steel arches – one for each victim. Each one celebrates the unique personality and nature of each person through personal tributes that reflect their interests and passions; for example, with metallic sculptures of cats and basketball nets.

The arches appear to change colour as they reflect the water, while through them you can see across to the west side of the river towards the crash site, to another installation consisting of 11 lights suspended on reeds.

The memorial sits next to the start of Downs Link, an atmospheric 59-km-long path which is open to walkers, horse riders and cyclists all year round. See p. 202 for details.

# ART DECO TERMINAL BUILDING AT BRIGHTON CITY AIRPORT ⑩

## *A reminder of a bygone era of aviation*

*Cecil Pashley Way, Shoreham-by-Sea, West Sussex, BN43 5FF*
*flybrighton.com*
*Weekdays 10am–3pm, weekends 12pm–3pm*
*Visitors are free to wander around inside*
*One-hour guided tours are available for small groups (minimum 6 people)*

Taking a flying lesson, enjoying a helicopter ride, chartering a private jet, or having tea at The Hummingbird café are the most common reasons for visiting Brighton City Airport.

There is another less obvious one, however: to have a snoop around its incredible Art Deco terminal building, which has featured in many films and TV programmes including *The Da Vinci Code* and Agatha Christie's *Poirot*.

Curious visitors are free to pop in for a wander around on their own, or take a tour run by airport volunteers, who will take you into the historic hangar and onto the runways. They also offer insights into how the airport operates today and its history, particularly during World War Two when it was used as a base for the then newly formed 277 Air Sea Rescue Squadron.

Shoreham Airport – as it was known when it was founded in 1910 – is the oldest airport in the UK, and the oldest purpose-built commercial airport in the world. Opened to the public in 1936, its iconic Art Deco terminal building was designed by a Brighton architect called Stavers Tiltman. What is remarkable about it is that most of its original Art Deco features remain intact, from the ceiling decorations down to the light switches and signage.

The airport was opened by an eccentric local portrait artist named Harold H Piffard, who went to Lancing College, which you can see across the runway (see p. 198). Piffard had enjoyed a number of intriguing jobs, having worked on a tea plantation in India, and as a member of an acrobatic troupe at home in England. One day, he decided to focus on a completely new hobby: aviation.

In 1910, he hand-built and flew his biplane at the airfield in Shoreham, where the airport now stands. It is said he learned to fly the biplane in order to win a crate of champagne from the landlord of the Sussex Pad Inn: if he could fly the plane over to collect the champagne, he could have it. He was successful, but had to walk the plane back as he yet had to learn how to turn it round, and so could not take off again. Soon after, Shoreham Airport became a popular aviation centre. The restaurant is named after Piffard's plane, *Hummingbird*.

Shoreham Airport was renamed Brighton City Airport when it was bought by a new owner in 2014.

# HOUSEBOATS OF SHOREHAM

⑪

## *An artistic collection of boats*

*Riverbank*
*Old Shoreham Road, Shoreham-by-Sea, East Sussex*
*Open to view from the outside only or during the Adur Festival*
*adurartcollective.co.uk*

On the banks of the River Adur in the coastal town of Shoreham-by-Sea is a distinctive collection of more than 50 houseboats. You will find them hidden along a towpath called Riverbank at the south end of a footbridge that links Shoreham's charming old town with Riverbank and nearby Shoreham Beach, with its atmospheric boardwalk through a rare shingle habitat (see p. 210).

The boats in the houseboat collective look more like flamboyant works of art than floating homes. You will know that you have found them when you start to notice all the incongruous features like old cars and rusty planes, and odd bits of bric-a-brac spilling out from the front gardens.

There is one with a rusty old coach on top of it, another with a Robin Reliant welded onto the side, and another designed to look like a Second World War bomber aeroplane complete with faux missiles. No two boats are the same.

It is fun to walk along the path and take in all the random details, and if you are local or visit Shoreham often, to watch the boats transform over time.

The Shoreham Houseboat community has a history that dates back to the 1920s, although the community grew considerably after the Second World War, as Britain faced a post-war accommodation shortage. It grew further in the 1960s and 70s when it became a popular place to live for those seeking an alternative lifestyle.

Some of the houses are set inside decommissioned military craft, for example. Two of them were once used during the D-Day landings (a British gunboat and a British landing craft), while a post-war German torpedo boat has been turned into a four-bedroom home.

Not all boats in the collective look are so outlandish in appearance. Rebus Stone, for example, is set inside an old bunker ship which has been hand-crafted over seven years into a stylish family home, with a pretty outside deck and a living roof. The Raft, next door, with its simple and modern design, has been completely hand built from scratch into a cosy home for two.

The Shieldsman, an old ferry which carried passengers between North and South Shields across the River Tyne in the north of England, was saved from a life as a floating disco and turned into a house complete with living room and two new bedrooms. A lower passenger deck is now a living area and kitchen.

## *Rent a houseboat*

If you are curious to know what the boats look like inside, some are available to rent on Airbnb.

The community is also the setting for a huge workshop and pop-up café, a community social space that hosts meditation, yoga, film nights, live music, markets, healing sessions and even a monthly pub night.

# SHOREHAM BEACH BOARDWALK ⑫

## *A little-known walkway through a unique coastal habitat*

*Shoreham Beach*
*Shoreham-by-Sea, East Sussex*

Brighton and Hove's beaches heave with visitors in summertime. Despite Shoreham's proximity to the city, however, somehow its atmospheric beach boardwalk escapes most tourists' radars. Even plenty of long-time local residents overlook it as a tranquil place for a stroll.

With its rare, vegetated shingle beach lined with modernist beach houses, it feels like you have stumbled on a wild and windswept beach in a south-western corner of Australia, or a part of Canada or California.

The Shoreham Beach Boardwalk starts (or ends) at Shoreham Fort and winds its way 1.5 km to Ferry Road close to Shoreham Village, through the unique coastal habitat of Shoreham Beach, which was declared a Local Nature Reserve in 2006 for its vegetated shingle, a globally rare and threatened habitat.

This type of habitat is defined as an area where specialised plants have adapted to survive harsh conditions on beaches, such as a lack of fresh water and nutrients, and exposure to wind and waves.

It is one of a handful of rare, vegetated shingle beaches in the south east of England (there is another in Sussex at Climping Beach, see p. 86). The largest is at Dungeness in Kent, home to 600 species of plants, which is a third of all plants found in the UK.

The Shoreham Beach Nature Reserve forms part of the newly created Brighton and Lewes Downs UNESCO World Biosphere Reserve called the Living Coast. The only Biosphere in the world to unite a marine and urban landscape, it is home to around 90 recorded species of rare plants (and counting), some of which are highlighted on information boards dotted along the boardwalk.

Late May or early June are good months to explore the area, when sea kale and red valerian bloom, followed by the yellow horned poppy, vibrant blue viper's bugloss and the golden daisy-like flowers on the silver ragwort. Particularly beautiful are the carpets of low-growing flowers, like pink ivy-leaved toadflax, thrift, white sea campions, kidney vetch and the rare starry clover.

## *Guided wildflower walks, rock pooling ...*

A group of volunteers called the Friends of Shoreham Beach manages the 26-hectare reserve. To promote their work maintaining this special environment, they organise various events throughout the year, such as guided wildflower walks in June when the beach is at its best, rock pooling in August when tides are low, and monthly beach clean-ups and sessions to monitor the different flora and fauna varieties. Visit fosbeach.com to get involved.

# SHOREHAM HARBOUR LIFEBOAT STATION TOUR ⑬

*Behind the scenes of a lifesaving rescue operation – as seen on TV*

*Kingston Beach*
*Brighton Road, Shoreham-by-Sea, West Sussex, BN43 6RN*
*01273 596376*
*Weekdays 10am–2pm, weekends 10am–4pm and during Heritage Open Days*
*Admission free but donations welcome*

For over 150 years, the work of the Royal National Lifeboat Institution at Shoreham Harbour has been incredible. All members of the lifeboat crew and shore helpers, apart from the full-time paid mechanic, are volunteers on call 24 hours a day, 365 days a year, ready to save lives at sea.

The institution receives no Government funding and relies on voluntary donations, legacies and money from fundraising activities.

Taking a tour is a great way to support the RNLI's vital work. It is also an opportunity for a behind-the-scenes look at life in the RNLI Shoreham Harbour Station, and a close-up look at its world-class lifeboat.

Tours are fun and are led daily by volunteer guides who take visitors round the £4 million state-of-the-art boathouse built in 2010. Designed around its lifeboat, it consists of a crew training room, wet kit drying room, changing room and public viewing platforms.

The tours start inside the boathouse on the top viewing platform, with an introduction to the star of the show, the £2.7 million Tamar-class lifeboat, the first of its kind in the RNLI's south-east region. Brought into service on 10 December 2010, the boat was purchased using gifts, legacies and a generous donation from a lady called Miss Enid Marjory Collett, whom the boat is named after.

Unfortunately, you cannot go inside it: understandably, when it is in the boathouse, it must remain ready to react to an emergency. Peppered with anecdotes and interesting facts about its design and technical ability, the lively nature of a tour makes up for any disappointment.

The boat is 16 metres long and five metres wide, has seven crew members, can hold a maximum of 118 people and has an unlimited towing capacity.

It is also equipped with CCTV to avoid litigation issues which occasionally sadly arise during rescue operations. This is also where footage for the BBC Two programme *Saving Lives at Sea* is taken from.

It is particularly surprising to learn about the survivors' room for 10 people hidden in the hull of the boat – you would never guess it was there.

Tours work their way down each level of the boathouse, through stairwells lined with old black and white pictures of the station and crew through time. They finish on the ground floor in the crew changing facilities for a look at the actual lifeboat crews' kit and where it is kept – and the chance to try it on.

### *See the lifeboat in action*

The Tamar lifeboat is launched on exercise most weeks, depending on operational needs and tide times. Visit shorehamlifeboat.co.uk for more information.

# HELP OUR KELP FORESTS

(14)

## *Magical disappearing underwater habitats*

*Help Our Kelp*
*Sussex Wildlife Trust*
*sussexwildlifetrust.org.uk/what-we-do/living-seas/kelp*

A swim in the sea off the Sussex coast, or pretty much anywhere in the UK, usually involves a complaint or two about seaweed. Soon, however, there could be no seaweed to moan about: these dense carpets of underwater plants are disappearing at an incredible rate.

Up until the 1980s, 60 square miles of well-established, dense kelp and seagrass forests – both types of seaweed – extended all along the Sussex coast, from Selsey to Brighton.

Today, only small pockets of these beautiful underwater landscapes remain. So much of it has been damaged by a combination of trawler fishing and dredging that the habitat is now in serious decline. There has also been a shift in distribution of these kelp forests around the country, which is thought to be due to climate change.

In 2019, Sussex Wildlife Trust, Blue Marine Foundation and the Marine Conservation Society initiated a campaign called Help Our Kelp. Launched by Sir David Attenborough, it hopes to restore a vast kelp forest off the Sussex coast in the first-ever marine kelp rewilding initiative.

The campaign supports a new bylaw proposed by the Sussex Inshore Fisheries and Conservation Authority (IFCA) to stop trawling within 4 km of the coast. Once the trawling management is in place, the partnership can move forward on plans to restore the forest. At the time of going to print, the campaign organisers had reported huge support for the bylaw and that they were currently waiting for the Secretary of State for the Environment at Defra to sign it. To keep up with the progress of the campaign, visit the website opposite.

Kelps are thought to have first appeared about 23 million years ago. They grow in large, dense groups, which form underwater forests. These large brown algae tend to grow in cold, rocky seafloors and are abundant in shallow waters around Britain's coastlines, sustaining a whole ecosystem.

Kelp forests are thought to be among the most productive and biodiverse places on earth. They support a huge variety of marine life such as seahorses, cuttlefish, lobster, sea bream and bass. They are important for our coastline as they break the flow of water, helping prevent coastal erosion, and can help prevent climate change.

Globally, kelp forests absorb 600 million tonnes of carbon which is roughly twice the amount of carbon that the UK emits per year, explains Dr Ian Hendy, Head of Science at Blue Marine Foundation, in a film made in conjunction with the campaign – you can find out about the campaign, and view the film using the link opposite.

# ART DECO INTERIOR OF THE DOME CINEMA

15

## *A beautifully preserved entertainment complex*

*The Dome Cinema*
*21-22 Marine Parade, Worthing, West Sussex, BN11 3PT*
*domecinema.co.uk*
*Open to view when you watch a film*

It is hard to concentrate on a film at The Dome in Worthing without being completely distracted by the original features of the auditorium, particularly the ornate ceiling: although it has been intricately restored, it looks almost as it would have done when it was first built in the early 1910s.

This unique Edwardian seaside entertainment complex is said to be one of the oldest working cinemas in England – just beaten by Brighton's Duke of York's Picture House, a city institution, which opened in 1910 (see *Secret Brighton: An Unusual Guide* by Jonglez publishing for more details).

While so many old cinemas around the country have disappeared, what is incredible about The Dome in Worthing is that it still exists and is in perfect condition. Somehow it survived some extremely hard times, including both world wars, changes in the entertainment industry, heavy competition from other local cinemas throughout the years and various local council redevelopment threats. It is also incredible that so many of its original features remain intact.

Its prospects improved in 1999, when the Worthing Dome and Regeneration Trust was awarded a Heritage Lottery Fund grant for a full restoration. This helped to restore the Dome to its original splendour, but also to modernise it with the latest cinema technology.

The building now contains two cinema screens, a café, bars, function rooms and two new retail units. The original tea rooms at the front of the building are also still open, filled with memorabilia reflecting the cinema's history, and you can visit these rooms separately (see p. 226).

Elsewhere, other original features include the beautiful polygonal ticket booth by the entrance, a wooden board showing film times, and the wood-panelled foyer, as well as the stunning ceiling in the downstairs screening room.

The Dome was opened in April 1911 by a Swiss impresario called Carl Adolf Seebold, as a multi-purpose entertainment hall known as The Kursaal. It was mainly used as a roller-skating rink, with live music and theatre. A tiny cinema called the Electric Theatre was added a few months later when Seebold opened a screening room upstairs which showed silent movies daily, and to which he played a piano accompaniment. This has now been restored and the original name has been kept.

The Kursaal was then renamed The Dome shortly after the outbreak of World War One in 1914, following a local competition which Seebold had initiated after deciding its original name sounded too Germanic.

As the cinema became more popular in the early 20th century, Seebold renovated the building to create a bigger screening room downstairs that would seat more people. The renovation was carried out by an architect called R. Kirksby for around £8,000, most of which remains as we see today.

# FORAGED BY FERN

⑯

## *Unique food tours and workshops*

*Based in Worthing, but guided foraging walks take place at various locations around Sussex*
*foragedbyfern.com*

Foraging guide, cook and forest schoolteacher, Fern Freud, runs entertaining guided foraging events and workshops around Sussex, which children and adults alike will enjoy. Her aim is to educate the public on safely identifying, sustainably gathering, and using the abundance of wild foods growing free on our doorsteps. What is fun about the workshops is that they are also peppered with forgotten stories and tales of folklore.

"Did you know that the mummified remains of a man who lived between 3,400 and 3,100 BC in Europe, known as Ötzi the Iceman, was found with two types of mushroom with leather strings through them, one of which we can still eat today? And that some of the first fishing nets ever made on the British Isles were woven from nettle fibres?", she says.

Fern's enlightening foraging courses take place all around the county from the seashore to the countryside. During a luxury coastal forage and beach spa day, for example, you will collect nutritious edible seaweeds to make into food and face masks, while on a gin workshop you will learn the secrets to harvesting wild botanicals and turning them into boozy concoctions.

Her interest in foraging started in childhood when her dad took her hunting for wild mushrooms. "It was a massive adventure because we knew it could be quite dangerous and we had no idea what we were going to find! We found mushrooms of all shapes and sizes, threw them into baskets and took them home to identify. We leafed through old dusty books and cut them and drew them and made notes on them, I remember feeling like a wise old botanist", she says.

Her journey to becoming a foraging guide happened organically after she started sharing stories of her adventures on social media. "I would post pictures of our journeys into the South Downs; baskets brimming with edible mushrooms, dinners and desserts we made with our finds when we got home. I would get lots of messages of curiosity and intrigue from friends of friends and others in my community, asking what I had and how I knew it was edible and most often if they could come with me on my next foraging walk", she explains.

Foraging sessions with Fern generally include a 2.5-hour guided foraging walk in which you will learn about a wide range of edible, medicinal and poisonous plants, followed by a small picnic or campfire lunch made of wild foods.

Private sessions can be tailored to individual interests – for example, if you have a particular interest in folklore, herbalism or a specific ingredient.

# SISTINE CHAPEL REPLICA CEILING ⑰

## *Away from the Vatican City crowds*

*English Martyrs Catholic Church*
*Goring Way, Goring-by-Sea, Worthing, East Sussex, BN12 4UH*
*01903 506890*
*english-martyrs.co.uk*
*April to October*
*Free but donations welcome*

English Martyrs Catholic Church in the quiet Sussex borough of Goring has a unique claim to fame: it is home to the only hand-painted copy of the world-famous ceiling of the Sistine Chapel in the Vatican City, Rome. A trip to Goring to see it is also the chance for tourist-trap-phobes to pretend they are looking at Michelangelo's 16th-century masterpiece without competing with the crowds.

What is also remarkable is how ordinary the English Martyrs Catholic Church looks from the outside. Set in a single-storey modern-brick building, you would be forgiven for driving straight past it without realising. There is little to indicate that it is a church, let alone the surprise waiting inside. Walk through the door, however, and look up above the simple wooden pews, laid out in bold yellows, greens, pinks and blues: you can see God dividing the land and waters, making the sun and earth, reaching out a powerful finger to spark life into Adam.

This version of the Sistine Chapel ceiling was hand-painted by local parishioner and sign writer Gary Bevans. He never went to art college but was nevertheless inspired to recreate Michelangelo's version after he went on a pilgrimage to Rome and was transfixed by the wonder of the chapel. He started it in 1987 and finished five years later.

Bevans tackled it by mapping the 30-metre painting on a grid. Then he fixed plywood panels to the ceiling, primed them in white and copied his drawing onto it, sometimes working by candlelight through the night to get it done. Sussex's Sistine is two-thirds the size of the original, and its proportions are exact, which makes it a mathematical feat as well as an artistic one.

Quirks to spot include the last supper oil painting, which has a parishioner standing at the back holding a chain of the incense burner, the priest's dog that died, Mary standing on the left and a small child with one of the apostles.

The ceiling is free to view but donations are welcome – these allow the church to help its parishioners by running programmes like groups for toddlers and lonely people.

While you are here, do not miss a vibrant stained-glass window at the south end of the church, which stands out from the rest with its modern design. It is made using glass recovered from a convent church in Littlehampton. It was designed by Annie Goodman, an architectural designer and historian, but made by her son, Jeremy Goodman, a professional glassmaker.

# MANOR ROAD GARAGE

⑱

## *A striking Art Deco reminder*

*17 Manor Road*
*East Preston,*
*West Sussex, BN16 1QA*

If there is one building that stands out among all the others in the Sussex village of East Preston, it is the old Manor Road Garage.

With its whitewashed Art Deco façade, its swaying palms and its perfectly preserved set of four brightly coloured Shell petrol pumps, it looks like it has been plucked straight from Miami in Florida, famous for its historic Art Deco architecture.

The Manor Road Garage dates back to 1919, when the central part of the workshop is said to have been built. It is thought to have been extended in 1930 by a firm called Boulton and Paul, and the façade added in 1934, although it is not known by whom.

According to Historic England, a 1937 estate agent's guide contains an advert for the Manor Road Garage giving details of sales, services, repairs, cars for hire and a garage with room for 50 cars.

It was a fully operational garage until 1973, and records show it was owned and run by a man called John Lillywhite. It remained closed and abandoned for almost 40 years: the whitewashed façade left to crumble, the original curved windows taken out and boarded up, the once gleaming forecourt becoming overgrown with weeds. It stayed like this until developers bought it in 2011, and discovered several vintage Rolls Royces, MGs, and a grey Massey Ferguson tractor inside, in various states of disrepair.

The building has since been converted into apartments, which saw the back of the building knocked down and rebuilt. The Art Deco façade was preserved and listed by Historic England along with the set of four petrol pumps which are thought to date back to the 1940s or early 1950s, and are considered rare. They light up at night.

Historically, the building represented three phases of early motoring, while the Art Deco frontage continues to be of architectural interest in that it is substantially intact.

The style now called Art Deco originated in France in the early 20th century. Its heyday was from 1920 to 1940 when it became widely known following the great *Exposition des Arts Decoratifs et Industriels Modernes* (*Exposition des Art Deco*, in short), held in Paris in 1925. Typical features include geometric and angular shapes, and fabrics like chrome, glass and mirrors.

Other examples of preserved Art Deco buildings in Sussex include the Worthing Dome (see p. 216) and Brighton City Airport, formerly known as Shoreham Airport (see p. 206).

# *Unusual Bars, Cafés and Restaurants*

# WORTHING TO HORSHAM

## ① THE PROJECTIONISTS BAR

*The Dome Cinema, 21-22 Marine Parade, Worthing, West Sussex, BN11 3PT*
*01903 823112 • domecinema.co.uk*
Nostalgic bar inside the preserved Dome Cinema decorated with old cinema memorabilia. Open to cinema and non-cinema goers.

## ② THE VINTAGE TEA ROOM

*The Dome Cinema, 21-22 Marine Parade, Worthing, West Sussex, BN11 3PT*
*01903 823112 •domecinema.co.uk*
Chintzy tea rooms within the Dome Cinema complex dating back to the early 1900s, filled with memorabilia reflecting the cinema's history (see p. 216). Serving all the usual tearoom fare. Open to cinema and non-cinema goers.

## ③ EAST BEACH CAFÉ

*Sea Road, Littlehampton, West Sussex, BN17 5GB*
*01903 731903 • eastbeachcafe.co.uk*
Architect-designed café resembling a giant piece of driftwood set on Littlehampton's sweeping East Beach. On the menu are upmarket versions of classic seaside food like fish and chips with pea purée, salt and pepper squid with chilli, and local wines.

## ④ THE HUMMINGBIRD CAFE

*Brighton City Airport, 5G Cecil Pashley Way, Shoreham-by-Sea, West Sussex, BN43 5FF*
*01273 452300 • facebook.com/thehummingbirdsussex/*
Traditional café with a terrace overlooking the runway of the first ever commercial airport in the country (see p. 206). Boasts an original Art Deco interior which can be seen throughout the building. All the café usuals like tea, coffee, cakes and light snacks are on offer, as well as Sunday roasts. They also cater for private events held at the airport.

## ⑤ RESTAURANT INTERLUDE

*Leonardslee Lake and Gardens, Brighton Road, Lower Beeding, Horsham, West Sussex, RH13 6PP*
*0871 8733 363 • leonardsleegardens.co.uk*
Michelin-starred restaurant set within a country house complete with its own vineyard. Serving tasting menus with 14 or 19 courses that change with the seasons. Dishes are made with ingredients foraged directly from the 240-acre Leonardslee Gardens, or ethically sourced from elsewhere in Sussex.

## ⑥ ARCHITECTURAL PLANTS CAFÉ

*Stane Street, North Heath, Pulborough, West Sussex, RH20 1DJ*
*07891 103444 • architecturalplants.com/architectural-cafe*
A café set inside a spectacular giant greenhouse within a nursery specialising in unusual, shapely and exotic plants. Everything on the menu is made using ingredients sourced from small independent businesses around Sussex, including the wines and beers. The fish finger sandwich with tartare sauce and crusty bread is particularly good.

### ⑦ TERRE DE SIENNE

*15 Chatsworth Road, Worthing, BN11 1LY*
*07872 394244 • terredesiennechocolate.com*
A delightful artisan chocolate shop serving creamy cups of hot chocolate made with their own bean-to-bar chocolates. Flavours include dark chocolate, ginger dark chocolate, chilli dark chocolate, pumpkin spice vegan 'milk' chocolate, hazelnut milk chocolate, white chocolate, cashew caramelised white chocolate, as well as a few vegan options. The menu also changes with the seasons.

## EASTBOURNE TO RYE

### ⑧ AG HENDY KITCHEN & DINING ROOMS

*36 High Street, Hastings, East Sussex, TN34 3ER*
*01424 447171 • aghendy.com/kitchen*
Open every weekend in the summer for lunch is this eccentric kitchen and dining room set inside the AG Hendy Homewares shop on Hastings' high street. It offers a set menu around seafood and vegetables, with a minimum order of two courses (see also p. 176).

### ⑨ BOULEVARD BOOKSHOP AND THAI CAFÉ

*32 George Street, Hastings, East Sussex, TN34 3EA*
*01424 436521 • thaicafeandbookshop.com*
Quaint bookshop in Hastings' old town by day, cosy bring-your-own Thai restaurant by night. It is owned and run by husband and wife team, Graham and Natthawan Frost, who welcome diners to browse the books while they wait for their delicious homemade Thai meal to be prepared. Open at weekends.

### ⑩ THE RYE WATERWORKS

*Tower Street, Rye, East Sussex, TN31 7AT*
*01797 224110 • ryewaterworks.co.uk*
A family-run micropub set inside a 300-year-old water pump house serving eight local ales, two keg beers and 12 local ciders along with a selection of wines, gins and soft drinks. Families, dogs and people just wanting to have a nose around are all welcome.

## CHICHESTER TO PETWORTH

### ⑪ NOTARIANNI'S MILK BAR AND RESTAURANT

*201-203 Terminus Road, Eastbourne, East Sussex, BN21 3DH*
*01323 723332*
Nostalgic diner-style café with a beautiful old shopfront run by the same Italian family since it opened in 1928. Serves all the British café classics like bacon sarnies and fried breakfasts, mugs of tea and coffee, as well as generous helpings of its delicious homemade Italian ice cream.

### ⑫ THE VINYL FRONTIER

*Little Chelsea, 35 Grove Road, Eastbourne, East Sussex, BN21 4TT*
*01323 410313 • facebook.com/vinylfrontierrecordshop/*

Drink coffee as you browse the vinyl at this cool independent record shop in Eastbourne's alternative shopping district, Little Chelsea (see p. 146) – described as the 'next wave of Coastal cool' by *The Sunday Times*. They also have a bar and host DJ nights, live music on Saturdays, quiz nights, and open mic poetry evenings.

### ⑬ MILL CAFÉ

*Stonecross Windmill, Beggars Lane, Stonecross, Pevensey, East Sussex, BN24 5EA*
*stonecrosswindmill.co.uk/cafe*

Tiny tearoom inside the former grain store of this working windmill. On offer are the usual café staples like tea and coffee – just £1 a cup – as well as cold drinks. Cakes and biscuits are homemade using flour freshly milled at the windmill, which is also for sale in here. All profits go towards the running and upkeep of the windmill.

### ⑭ GOODWOOD AERODROME CAFÉ

*Goodwood Aerodrome, The Goodwood Motor Circuit, Chichester, West Sussex, PO18 0PH*
*goodwood.com/stay-dine-relax/restaurants/aerodrome-cafe/*

Sleek new café overlooking Goodwood Airfield serving snacks and light lunches. On sunny and good-weather days, head up to the rooftop viewing platform to watch the aircraft from the flight school take off and land (see also p. 80).

### ⑮ MOTOR CIRCUIT CAFÉ

*Goodwood Motor Circuit, Chichester, West Sussex, PO18 0PH*
*01243 755167 • goodwood.com/stay-dine-relax/restaurants/motor-circuit-cafe/*

Nostalgic-styled café set inside a former control tower overlooking the Goodwood racetrack serving a traditional British lunch menu. The walls are lined with pictures of bygone days of racing at Goodwood. On sunny days, head to the balcony to watch the activity on the motor circuit.

### ⑯ NAAFI WAGON TAKEAWAY CAFÉ

*Goodwood Motor Circuit, Chichester, West Sussex, PO18 0PH*

An old wartime NAAFI wagon has been turned into a takeaway food van which can be found in the paddock car park. Serving favourites like bacon and sausages sandwiches, burgers and baguettes made using organic produce from the Goodwood farm, as well as hot and cold drinks. The van was originally used by NAAFI which stands for The Navy, Army and Air Force Institutes; a company created by the British Government on 9 December 1920 to run recreational establishments needed by the British Armed Forces, and to sell goods to servicemen and their families.

## ⑰ THE BOX CAFÉ

*Kinsbrook Vineyard, Picketty Corner, West Chiltington Road, West Chiltington, West Sussex, RH20 2LT*
*kinsbrookvineyard.com*

Drinks and snacks, including Kinsbrook wines and little plates for pairing, are served at The Box Café belonging to this new boutique vineyard on the Sussex scene. Kinsbrook also hosts vineyard tours twice a week, and has a vineyard walking trail. See p. 235 for more information.

## ⑱ TERRACE BAR

*Upperton Vineyards, Upperton Farm, Tillington, Petworth, West Sussex, GU28 0RD*
*01798 343695 • uppertonvineyards.co.uk*

An atmospheric outdoor terrace bar on the Upperton Vineyard, boasting incredible views over the vineyard and across to the South Downs. Come to enjoy an Upperton sparkling wine served by the glass or bottle, local Langham Brewery beer and Sussex cheese platters. Open from 12 to 5pm Friday and Saturday.

## ⑲ ARUNDEL JAILHOUSE

*The Undercroft, Maltravers Street, Arundel, West Sussex, BN18 9AP*
*arundeljailhouse.co.uk*

Unique live entertainment venue in the former Arundel Town Hall Prison, originally built in 1836 to house inmates convicted in the upstairs courthouse. Every weekend it transforms at night into an underground club for live music, comedy and theatre – such as murder mystery dinners, jazz and blues nights, and retro discos. It is also said to be haunted and regularly visited by many paranormal groups for investigation.

## ⑳ THE OLD RAILWAY STATION TEAROOMS

*The Old Station, Station Road, Petworth, GU28 0JF*
*01798 342346 • old-station.co.uk*

Set within the former waiting room of the old Petworth Railway station which is now a unique hotel. It offers the usual English café staples like cream teas and sandwiches, which you can enjoy inside by the fire or on the platform in sunny weather. Booking is encouraged.

## ㉑ HORSE GUARDS INN

*Upperton Road, Tillington, West Sussex, GU28 9AF*
*01798 342 332 • thehorseguardsinn.co.uk*

Relaxed, friendly and unconventional local village pub dating back 350 years. In winter, you can roast chestnuts foraged from Petworth Park on one of the open log fires, play board games at the bar and drink warm spiced cider. On sunnier days, enjoy the herb-filled garden while slumped in a deckchair with a Pimm's, or have lunch at a shady table.

# LEWES TO GLYNDE

### ㉒ CAFÉ DU JARDIN

*15 Malling Street, Lewes, East Sussex, BN7 2RA*
*01273 480777 • cafedujardin.co.uk*

French-inspired café with a unique setting in the bric-a-brac filled courtyard of the quirky Pastorale Antiques. Browse the stacks before ordering a hot frothy cappuccino and a classic croque monsieur or steak frites. They also have a wine cellar which is open on Friday and Saturday evenings for drinks and hors d'oeuvres.

### ㉓ FIRE + WILD

*The woods, somewhere near Lewes, East Sussex*
*fireandwild.co.uk*

A dining and events company with a twist – every few months, they transform a secret woodland location close to their base in Lewes, East Sussex, into the magical setting for an epic intimate outdoor banquet inspired by nature and the seasons. See p. 26 for more details.

# BURGESS HILL TO ALFRISTON

### ㉔ WILDFLOUR CAFÉ

*Saddlescombe Farm, Saddlescombe Road, Poynings, East Sussex, BN45 7DE*
*wildflourcafe.co.uk*

Vegetarian café set in a shady courtyard at Saddlescombe Farm. Everything is homemade and baked on site in the kitchen set inside a renovated 1961 Carlight caravan – the courtyard centrepiece. Open seasonally from March to October.

### ㉕ BEANSTALK TEA GARDEN

*The Old Coach Road, Lewes, East Sussex, BN8 6PA*
*facebook.com/BeanstalkTeaGarden/*

It does not get more English country garden tea room than at this unique venue. Set at the foot of the South Downs on the Firle Estate, it offers a homely atmosphere and a peaceful and tranquil setting for traditional cream teas, home-made cake and other snacks made with local ingredients. There is also an Indian tea tent and roaming peacocks.

### ㉖ SECRET SUSSEX SUPPERCLUB

*facebook.com/secretsupperclubsociety/*

Atmospheric and convivial seasonal supper clubs held in beautiful and unusual locations around East and West Sussex, such as the Trotton Estate Vineyard (see p. 235) and the Architectural Plants Café (see p. 226).

1

6

9

TOWER ST
10

NOTARIANNIS
MILK BAR
11

CAFÉ
DU JARDIN
22

# *Hidden vineyards*

Sussex offers the perfect conditions and soil for growing grapes needed to make sparkling wine. Not surprisingly, many big names in British sparkling wine are based here, but there are also lots of smaller, lesser-known boutique wineries and vineyards scattered around the county, which offer tours, tastings and vineyard trails, and make the ideal setting for a summer picnic.

# EAST SUSSEX

### ① BEACON DOWN VINEYARD

*Browns Lane, Cross-in-Hand, Heathfield, East Sussex, TN21 0QJ*
*07870 851138 • beacondown.co.uk*

A family-run boutique winery in the High Weald offering relaxed tours which include a leisurely walk around the vineyard, an introduction to the challenge of producing British sparkling wine, and a tasting session. Alternatively, the vineyard is open to visitors at the weekend in spring and summer if you just fancy a wander and a picnic – bring your own or order one to enjoy with some wine.

### ② BLACK DOG HILL

*17–19 High Street, Ditchling, Hassocks, East Sussex, BN6 8SY*
*07710 572974 • blackdoghillvineyard.com*

Three generations of the same family run this intriguing sounding vineyard named after a ghostly black dog which legend says roams the area bearing the souls of the departed to their resting place in the next world. It does not offer tours, but it has a shop in the nearby village of Ditchling where you can enjoy tasting its range of award-winning sparkling classic cuvée wines.

### ③ COURT GARDENS FARM

*Orchard Lane, Ditchling, East Sussex, BN6 8TH*
*01273 844 479 • courtgarden.com/vineyard-and-winery-tours*

Open since 2005, tours of this family-run vineyard include an introduction to the operation, a walk around the vineyard, a visit to the winery and a tasting in which you have three choices: Court Garden sparkling wines, Court Garden award-winning wines and cheese, or the English sparkling wine, Prosecco and Champagne taste off. They also host pop-up opera nights in their barn in summer.

### ④ WILDWOOD VINEYARD

*Eridge Road, Eridge, East Sussex, TN3 9EQ*
*07970 155303 • wildwoodvineyard.co.uk*

Not far from the mysterious Eridge Rocks (see p. 136) is this family-run vineyard named after a nearby shaw of ancient wild woodland. Hear the story of their wine-making adventures, followed by a glass or two in the vineyard on a laid-back tour. They also offer visitors the chance to adopt a vine or join the harvest which takes place over three separate weekends in October. Private tours can be organised, too.

# WEST SUSSEX

## ⑤ KINSBROOK VINEYARD

*Picketty Corner, West Chiltington Lane, West Chiltington, West Sussex, RH20 2LT*
*01403 741967 • kinsbrookvineyard.com*

New boutique vineyard on the Sussex scene hosting vineyard tours twice a week. There is also a vineyard walking trail that visitors are free to wander alone. Drinks and snacks, including Kinsbrook wines and little plates for pairing, are served at The Box Café. There are also plans to open accommodation on the site in the future.

## ⑥ REDFOLD VINEYARDS

*Nutbourne Lane, Nutbourne, West Sussex, RH20 2HS*
*01798 813657 • ambrielsparkling.com/about-us/vineyards/*

Discover the setting for Ambriel sparkling wines on a private tour and tasting which can be arranged by appointment. Tours include a walk around the vines surrounding a wildlife corridor. The vines are also grazed by the owner's golden Guernsey goats and flock of ouessants – the smallest sheep in the world – in winter.

## ⑦ TROTTON ESTATE VINEYARD

*Gatehouse Lane, Trotton, Petersfield, West Sussex, GU31 5DA*
*07787 510383 • trottonestatevineyards.com*

A fascinating small vineyard set on fields once home to the owners' now retired polo ponies, some of whom you might still see wandering around. Tours are casual, fun and informative and introduce you to the estate wines which you taste as you walk through the vines. Tours run every Saturday from May to September. Special dates can be arranged on request.

## ⑧ UPPERTON

*Upperton Farm, Tillington, Petworth, West Sussex, GU28 0RD*
*01798 343695 • uppertonvineyards.co.uk*

Gather 10 or more friends and vineyard owner, Andy Rogers, will take you on a private tour of his vineyard, explain how it is run and how sparkling wine is made. Tours end with a tasting session in either the terrace bar or the shop, depending on when you visit. Tours can take place on Tuesday to Thursday at any time; Friday and Saturday at 5.30pm.

It was September 1995 and Thomas Jonglez was in Peshawar, the northern Pakistani city 20 kilometres from the tribal zone he was to visit a few days later. It occurred to him that he should record the hidden aspects of his native city, Paris, which he knew so well. During his seven-month trip back home from Beijing, the countries he crossed took in Tibet (entering clandestinely, hidden under blankets in an overnight bus), Iran and Kurdistan. He never took a plane but travelled by boat, train or bus, hitchhiking, cycling, on horseback or on foot, reaching Paris just in time to celebrate Christmas with the family.

On his return, he spent two fantastic years wandering the streets of the capital to gather material for his first "secret guide", written with a friend. For the next seven years he worked in the steel industry until the passion for discovery overtook him. He launched Jonglez Publishing in 2003 and moved to Venice three years later.

In 2013, in search of new adventures, the family left Venice and spent six months travelling to Brazil, via North Korea, Micronesia, the Solomon Islands, Easter Island, Peru and Bolivia. After seven years in Rio de Janeiro, he now lives in Berlin with his wife and three children.

Jonglez Publishing produces a range of titles in nine languages, released in 40 countries.

## ACKNOWLEDGEMENTS

A huge thank you to everybody who supported and listened to me talk endlessly about this epic project; to those who recommended places to visit, gave local insights and helped me with my research; my friends and family for their constant encouragement; Lyndsey and her partner, Lee, for their unwavering enthusiasm; my husband Dan for giving up his weekends to navigate me around Sussex; my Dad and friend, Barbara, for taking time out to explore with me; and all at JonGlez for the opportunity to fulfil a life-long dream to write a travel guidebook.

## PHOTOGRAPHY CREDITS

All photos by **Lyndsey Haskell** except:
Dark Sky Sites © South Downs National Park Authority
Browne Burial Ground © Ellie Seymour
Lewes Land Nature Reserve © Emma Croman
Glyndebourne Backstage Tours © Charlotte Boulton
Glyndebourne Pugs © Sam Stephenson
Bow Bells milestone marker © creative commons
Farleys House and Gallery, Tony Tree © Lee Miller Archives, England 2020. All rights reserved. leemiller.co.uk
Surrealist Picnic, Tony Tree © Lee Miller Archives, England 2020. All rights reserved. leemiller.co.uk
Duncan Grant's Studio © Penelope Fewster
Racton Ruin © Lyall Pratt
Sherlock Holmes' Fictional Home © Ellie Seymour
The Cable Hut © Ellie Seymour
Beeding Toll House © Alison Avery
Sistine Chapel Replica Ceiling © Lyall Pratt
The Potager © Ellie Seymour
The Tower Room © Fiona, London Unattached
Wild Sussex © Alun Callender
Peregrine falcons of Chichester Cathedral © David Shaw
Millennium Seed Bank © RBG Kew
Hammerwood Park © David Pinnegar
Relics of the Royal Observatory Greenwich © Andrew Hasson, Alamy
Remains of John 'Butcher' Breads © Rye Town Council
Knepp © Knepp Wildland
Shoreham Harbour Lifeboat Station Tour © Shoreham RNLI
Handling Birds of Prey © Vit Baisa, Dreamstime
Help Our Kelp forests © Andy Jackson, Sussex Wildlife Trust

**Cartography:** Cyrille Suss – **Design:** Emmanuelle Willard Toulemonde – **Editing:** Sigrid Newman – **Proofreading:** Kimberly Bess – **Publishing:** Clémence Mathé


Registration of copyright: April 2021 – Edition: 01
ISBN: 978-2-36195-462-8
Printed in Bulgaria by Dedrax